T0267934

THE UNIVERSITY OF ARKANSAS PRESS

SERIES IN BUSINESS HISTORY

VOLUME THREE

J. B. Hunt

The Long Haul to Success

Marvin Schwartz

The University of Arkansas Press
Fayetteville 1992

23 22 21 20   5 4 3

ISBN: 978-1-55728-250-7 (cloth)
ISBN: 978-1-68226-141-5 (paper)
e-ISBN: 978-1-61075-211-4

This book was designed by John Coghlan using the New Baskerville typeface

The paper used in this publication meets the minimum requirements of the American National Standard for Permanence of Paper
for Printed Library Materials Z39.48-1984. ⊛

Library of Congress Cataloging-in-Publication Data

Schwartz, Marvin, 1948-
    J.B. Hunt: the long haul to success / Marvin Schwartz.
        p.   cm. – (The University of Arkansas Press series in
    business history ; v. 3)
    Includes bibliographical references and index.
    ISBN 1-55728-250-1 (cloth: alk. paper)
    1. J.B. Hunt and Company–History. 2. Hunt, Johnnie Bryan, 1927-.
    3. Businessmen–United States–Biography. 4. Trucking–United
    States–History. I. Title. II. Series.
HE5623.Z7J647   1992

CONTENTS

INTRODUCTION

In the trucking industry today, the key word is "logistics." Formerly applied to a range of distribution activities, logistics now relates to the total service and support mechanisms a trucking company assigns its customers. In the 1990s, it has become the essential factor for a firm's ultimate success or failure.

Originally, logistics referred to a branch of military science related to the moving, supplying, and quartering of troops. In trucking, a similar degree of strategy and tactics is applied. Behind the front lines of the commercial market battlefield exists an extensive network of manufacturing and distribution centers.

The average consumer has little involvement with these factories and warehouses and has minimal exposure to the complex system for transporting goods or the critical efficiency imposed on that movement by a highly competitive marketplace. Consumers want their products on the market shelf or the showroom floor when they are ready to buy. Manufacturers must now compete not only on product price and quality but also on how quickly they can get a product to market or service their customer needs.

A new emphasis on speed-to-market or just-in-time manufacturing systems has placed greater demands on trucking services. A firm will have a distinct advantage if it can provide real time tracking of freight, if it can tell a shipper exactly where a load is and when it will be delivered. The technology to do this requires a satellite system that transmits data from the in-route truck to the carrier's mainframe computer.

More traditional aspects of carrier quality and reliability have also been upgraded. Logistics now require that carriers work with shippers to eliminate problem areas and provide equipment when and where it is needed, often on a national scale. Trucking firms that fail to meet a shipper's needs for individualized service may find themselves excluded from a narrowing group of selected carriers.

These operational demands on modern trucking firms are relatively unknown by the general public. What the public does know, especially when driving on the nation's interstate highway system, is that a seemingly endless stream of tractor-trailer rigs, the formidable "eighteen wheelers," has become a distinct presence on the American landscape.

Accompanying these vehicles is a perceived subculture whose artifacts include country music, diesel-pumping truck stops, CB radios, and the cliché image of the big rig driver in cowboy hat, boots, and shiny belt buckle.

This stereotype has been built on over-the-road drivers, but it ignores the fact that less than half of the 2.6 million professionals on the road today are long-haul drivers working for truckload carriers. The trucking industry also includes a great many less-than-truckload (LTL) carriers whose drivers, often members of the Teamsters Union, usually have short runs of 250 miles or less.

But public impressions are slow to change. The trucking industry has been dramatically restructured in recent years. Most of the changes followed the Federal Motor Carrier Act, 1980 legislation that deregulated the industry and allowed a fiercely competitive environment to develop.

Trucking deregulation has had mixed reviews, receiving

praise from companies that succeeded in the deregulated environment and predictable criticism from firms who have fared poorly or gone bankrupt. While the ultimate economic impact of that landmark legislation is still a matter of debate, one outcome is absolutely clear. Since 1980, J. B. Hunt Transport, Inc., has emerged as the largest, most efficient, and most profitable truckload firm in the nation.

From its corporate headquarters at Lowell, Arkansas, the Hunt operation includes a network of fifteen truck terminals and thirty-two shuttle yards. The corporate fleet of more than 4,700 tractors and 10,500 trailers drove an average forty-seven million miles per month in 1990, employing nearly six thousand drivers in the process. Revenue that year climbed to a record $579.8 million, and Hunt has repeatedly led the industry in operating ratio, an evaluation that relates cost to income and measures a company's overall business efficiency.

Hunt's success is closely linked to deregulation. The opportunities afforded by a deregulated industry are so similar to the operational history of J. B. Hunt that a senior information officer at the American Trucking Associations in Washington, D.C., suggested that the Hunt story was in itself the story of trucking deregulation. To fully understand deregulation, he said, one had only to analyze the Hunt performance.

Even more remarkable, the company did not begin to focus solely on trucking services until 1983. Before then, trucking was just one division, and a consistently unprofitable one, within The J. B. Hunt Company, an agricultural supply business started in 1961 at Stuttgart, Arkansas, business center for the nation's most dense rice-producing region.

Outside of Arkansas, few people know much about the early days of The J. B. Hunt Company. Business analysts are aware that the northwest corner of the state has been the breeding ground for several corporations of national prominence. A few miles north of Lowell, the retail giant Wal-Mart maintains its sprawling corporate headquarters at Bentonville. Immediately to the south at Springdale is Tyson Foods, the world's largest poultry company.

The question frequently asked is how Arkansas was able to produce these corporate leaders. In a state traditionally ranked among the lowest in the nation in per capita income and education, a rural state hard hit by the Depression and relatively bypassed by the economic prosperity of post-war America, what has given rise to such a concentration of entrepreneurial excellence?

A model for trucking deregulation, J. B. Hunt Transport is also the epitome of individual achievement. The life story of its founder, Johnnie Bryan Hunt, embodies the American rags-to-riches fable in its most engaging personification. Here is the Horatio Alger myth played out on a southern stage, its central character brimming with optimism and vitality. Hunt has been characterized as "reminiscent of the Texas oil tycoons of the 1950s and 1960s, a hearty humorous breed who believe pedigrees were for livestock."[1]

Friends call Hunt a man of unlimited vision and imagination, a promoter of ideas, one of the world's great salesmen. These qualities have led the company to prominence. They also distinguish Hunt as an individual. Talking to a group of new drivers, Hunt will relate his life story as an inspirational example, motivating the employees to believe, as he does, that a man can get anything he wants if he dedicates himself to a goal.

In 1988 when *Forbes* magazine listed him among the wealthiest four hundred people in the nation, Hunt was one of nine on the list with no high-school diploma. Finishing high school was never a consideration for Hunt. The child of poor sharecroppers, he picked cotton during his elementary-school years and left school after the seventh grade to work in his uncle's sawmill at Edgemont, Arkansas. It was 1939, and the twelve-year-old boy earned about $1.50 a day.

Nearly twenty years later, Hunt had the inspiration that would lead to his first major business success. He was a truck driver at the time, working an east Arkansas route that brought him through the Stuttgart rice fields. Piles of rice hulls, discarded from the local mills, were being burned in the fields. Smoke from the burning rice hulls clouded the sky. Hunt's idea had the simplicity found in many strokes of genius. Instead of burning the hulls, he devised a way to put them to use. Rice hulls have a light, spongy consistency that makes an ideal base litter for poultry houses. That same light density, however, had been a barrier to cost efficient transport. Hunt's contribution was a unique system of pressure packing the hulls in bags. Within a few years, The J. B. Hunt Company was the world's largest producer of rice hulls for poultry litter.

Hunt's new fortune allowed him to indulge his lifelong passion of business speculation. Under the umbrella of the rice-hull business, Hunt invested in several ventures. Some turned a fair profit. Some were outright losers. J. B. Hunt has suggested that potential acquisitions for his firm would be companies with a little risk to them, "something that would be fun."

For J. B. Hunt, the real joy is not so much in winning but in simply playing the game. "It's not the catch that satisfies me," he says, "it's the chase."

This eagerness to confront opportunity has brought many speculative ventures to Hunt's door. Johnelle Hunt, a pragmatic business partner throughout their forty-year marriage, recalls a standing joke from the early years about an imaginary sign outside the corporate headquarters that advertised, "Anyone with crazy ideas, stop here. We'll listen."

The willingness to listen gave rise to the trucking business. In 1969, Hunt acted on the suggestion of a rice-hull customer and bought a handful of used trucks and refrigerated trailers. Within the strictly regulated trucking industry at that time, the vehicles held little potential for profit. To Hunt, the fledgling truckline was too promising an opportunity to overlook.

In the 1990s, Hunt continues to find no shortage of new opportunities. In his executive office, he stands beside a four-foot-tall globe and points out new locations of seemingly obvious potential. Hunt smiles as he talks, and his easy laughter quickly engages even the most reticent audience. His personal enthusiasm is contagious, and its influence has permeated the corporate ranks. One executive has suggested that Hunt motivated people to view work as a privilege rather than an obligation.

"When you're having fun at a job, it's easy to enjoy what you do," the fellow said. Then he added what might be the unofficial corporate motto at J. B. Hunt: "I'd rather wear out than rust out anytime."

Like his associates Sam Walton and Don Tyson, Hunt has mixed a Depression-era work ethic with an unfailing self-confidence and a bold strategic vision. Arkansas has given rise to a cadre of businessmen with the rare ability to restructure the real world, to link seemingly unrelated parts and achieve a new working order whose simplicity is one of its most marvelous facets.

Hunt credits his corporate achievement to several external factors. He has consistently relied on a well-educated and skilled management team to turn his visionary concepts into reality. He has also been strongly influenced by Johnelle, an astute woman whose practical sense of business and world affairs has been an invaluable balance to her husband's creative spontaneity.

Yet for Hunt, the true foundation of his success is spiritual guidance. He is a devout Christian who reads the Bible every morning, a book he completes and starts over about every eighteen months. Hunt has called the Bible "God's road map for man," and he can cite specific passages that served as timely and accurate guides to decisions in his life.

With the Arkansas hill dialect still evident in his speech, Hunt will teach a local church Sunday-school class or host an international business conference. He will drink coffee with drivers at truck stops because it keeps him in touch with basic views, but also because he enjoys their company. He will encourage his own drivers to uphold standards of family and personal morality.

Back in his truck-driving days, Hunt had a standard reply

for anyone asking about his most recent trip. "Every trip is a good trip," he would say. "I haven't had a bad day since I stopped picking cotton."

This infectious optimism has been consistent throughout his life. Over the years, Hunt has not altered his values or priorities. His willingness to take on new business risks has not diminished. Friends insist that despite his personal fortune and enormous corporate influence, he is the same man he was years ago.

Hunt has been called the "image of the company." But J. B. Hunt Transport, by far the most successful of Hunt's many ventures, is not the full measure of the man. Unlike the public's impression of truck drivers, Hunt is a man who is truly all he appears to be. There are no hidden agendas. The surprising truth is the truth itself, that a man can overcome life's many obstacles without pretense or false understanding of his abilities, qualities common to all men of integrity.

Hunt's stamp of distinction can be seen in the yellow corporate logo that marks a vast truck fleet traveling the nation's highways.

1

Corporate History to 1980

Life in Cleburne County, the rural heartland of Arkansas, followed traditional patterns in 1927. There was work for those who wanted it in the logging woods and at the saw-mills. For those without land of their own, cleared fields could be rented for sharecropping. Outside the county seat at Heber Springs, small communities maintained a social order through the country church and one-room school house.

For Walter and Alma Hunt, a local couple whose third child, Johnnie Bryan, was born that year, 1927 was most likely near the end of a period of relative prosperity. During the Depression years that followed, four more children would be born and the family would struggle to provide for their needs.

It was a common experience at the time. For country people, the Depression did not dramatically affect their basic sustenance of food and shelter, most of which they provided for themselves. The lean years of the 1930s required people to work harder, but the ability to work hard was a personal resource most Arkansans of that era possessed.

Family values were enforced by Alma Hunt while Walter worked long hours, often pre-dawn until after dark, six or seven days a week. J. B. Hunt said some of his earliest memories are of his father drilling for oil in Cleburne County. That speculative venture yielded little financial return, but a clear work ethic had been established for the six Hunt sons.

"We were brought up in the Depression. It had always been there, so we didn't know it was bad times," J. B. Hunt said. "Father thought everything had to be done by good, hard work. We were all workaholics. It was all we knew."

Abandoning the oil well, Walter Hunt moved the family to his brother Wilburn's farm where they rented land and began sharecropping. They later relocated to Mississippi County in eastern Arkansas, sharecropping there as well. Cotton was the main cash crop at the time. Like many other families on their social level, the Hunts worked on land they did not own, earning the meager wages that bought their clothes and supplies. J. B. also worked in the cotton fields. He had little opportunity to keep up at school.

In the late 1930s, the family returned to Cleburne County and Walter Hunt began work for his brother's timber company. Walter worked at several "ground hog" sawmills, semi-portable operations in remote logging areas. Mill workers generally lived in tents at the site. J. B. Hunt said he grew up skinning logs and hauling them to the mill by horse and wagon.

"We had an old truck to haul the rough-cut lumber to town, and my five brothers and sister, we all learned to drive it," Hunt said. "At night, after everyone went home, we'd haul the lumber for free just to be able to go to town."

A Seventh-Grade Dropout

For Hunt, the sawmill, not the classroom, held immediate potential for helping to support the family. He quit school after the seventh grade and went to work full time for his uncle. During his teenage years, Hunt earned the same wage as the adults who worked in the mill, about $1.50 a day for twelve hours' work.

Hunt never returned to school. As an adult, his dropout status serves as an ironic contrast to his tremendous business success, but for Hunt, the true sacrifice of leaving school early in life has nothing to do with education.

"The real problem is that you don't grow up with people your own age," he said. "Think about a guy, twelve years old, who goes to work with all adults. Years later, all your dear friends have been dead a long time. You're thirty-five and your best friend is sitting in a rocking chair, an old man."

Working at the mill offered Hunt a real-world education that school could never provide. With the limited resources of a planer mill in a small Arkansas town, Hunt first showed the creative ingenuity he would apply a few years later in business.

A planer mill produces large quantities of wood shavings as it smoothes the edges of rough-cut boards. Every day, farmers came to the Heber Springs mill and shoveled the shavings into their trucks for use as poultry-house litter. Because the farmers did the work, there was no charge for the shavings.

"I could see that was a going business," Hunt said. "So I had my uncle's carpenter build this big house on stilts. We turned the blower vents to send the shavings up there. Now when the farmers came in, we'd just pull the lever and fill up the whole truck for four dollars a load. I got to making twelve dollars a day selling shavings and four dollars a day working. So I had floated up in the finance world."

Hunt worked in the mill and drove the lumber truck until he joined the army in 1945. His older brothers had already enlisted, and Hunt had been eager to join them throughout the war years. Military service offered tremendous exposure for the eighteen-year-old. At a Walgreen's Drug Store in Little Rock, Hunt found it was "so cold you could hardly stand it." The Cleburne County native had discovered air conditioning.

During the war, Alma Hunt became ill and required full-time nursing. The family doctor knew the Hunts could not afford such care, so he arranged for the Red Cross to bring J. B. Hunt back from his Kentucky base camp to tend to his mother in the hospital. Hunt spent several months of his military service stationed at the Searcy hospital.

When the war ended, Hunt was recruited for officers' training school. He declined the opportunity. Many years later, the corporate chairman still recognizes the error of that decision.

"It would have been a great opportunity," he said. "I wanted to join the army because everyone else had gone, but after the war was over, the glamour had passed. It just seemed I would be involved in a dead-end situation."

Rules of the Road

Returning to Heber Springs in 1947, J. B. Hunt resumed his position at the mill, but he also began hauling finished lumber. By this time, Walter Hunt had begun operating small sawmills and bringing his boards to Wilburn's planer mill. J. B. and his brothers picked up the retail end of the business, loading a truck with surplus boards and selling them wherever they could.

Hunt began selling in Arkansas, Missouri, and Illinois, staying gone a week or more at a time. Dealing with small lumber yards and building-supply companies, he learned that success in sales was as much a matter of personality as it was of product.

"That was a great education to become a super salesman," he said. "I learned to pull every trick in the book, to do whatever I had to do to survive."

Hunt recalled a steady customer who wouldn't accept two truckloads brought him from the Heber Springs mill because his lumberyard was overstocked. Hunt couldn't make the sale, but he stayed on to chat with the fellow. When the man teased him about being a bachelor, Hunt saw an opening.

"I lied and said I was going to get married the next night if I could get this load sold and get home," Hunt said. "He opened the gates and took both loads. Of course, every time I'd go back up there he'd ask me how my wife was. I was in terrible shape."

Hunt didn't limit himself to driving a lumber truck during this period. He was also working with area poultry growers, buying live chickens and trucking them to the Swift company's packing plant in Dexter, Missouri. Another local businessman involved in poultry was Johnie DeBusk, an affluent Heber Springs merchant and owner of Red River Feed Company, the only feed mill in town.

In 1948, Hunt decided to change careers, and he enrolled in an auctioneering school at Mason City, Iowa. The newly graduated auctioneer returned to Heber Springs and, with a cousin, borrowed the money to purchase the local livestock sale barn. The auction business did not work out, and Hunt was $3,600 in debt by the time he abandoned it.

Returning to trucking, Hunt sold lumber on the road and delivered poultry. But long-term prospects were slim in Heber Springs, so Hunt set his sights on Little Rock. Borrowing ten dollars from a friend, Hunt hitchhiked to Little Rock, leaving behind what must have seemed an insurmountable debt and a promising relationship with Johnie DeBusk's attractive daughter, Johnelle.

The Poorest Guy in the County

When Johnelle first met Hunt, he had just returned from auctioneer school. She said he talked so fast at the time she could hardly understand anything he said. One thing absolutely clear, however, was Hunt's financial status, a condition that must have given Johnie DeBusk some second thoughts.

"Here I was, this twenty-one-year-old truck driver, the

poorest guy in the county, dating this sixteen-year-old girl, one of the wealthiest girls in town," Hunt said. "That was the way we started. I always felt her folks liked me as a person, but it was kind of a long shot for this guy who couldn't read or write, working for four dollars a day. This guy's going to marry my daughter?"

Johnelle had the advantages of an education and a cultured home life. She had taken piano lessons, and her family was active in the local school and church. She had plans to attend college and become a teacher.

DeBusk had known the Hunt family for years. Like other country folks, they bought supplies at his general mercantile store. DeBusk's first encounter with his future son-in-law had been when Walter and Alma Hunt brought their six-month-old child into town to be weighed on the store scales.

Some years later, Johnelle was to hear about Hunt before actually meeting him. All of Heber Springs probably heard about Hunt driving his truck off the swinging bridge at Tumbling Shoals and crashing down the bank to the Little Red River below. Slashing his hand on the windshield, Hunt was unable to drive for a while, so his uncle gave him the job of exercising a horse he had purchased. Johnelle recalls first seeing Hunt riding past her house with his hand in a sling.

Johnelle met Hunt one evening when she and her friends all climbed aboard his sale-barn cattle truck for a ride through town. Johnelle said Hunt drove each of the girls home, but he took her home last.

"The next night when he stopped in the courthouse square again, we all started running to the truck," Johnelle said. "I outran everybody to sit next to him, and I guess I just stayed there. We dated for almost five years before we were married."

Johnelle recalled some dates didn't take place in very romantic settings. Hunt sometimes took her along on evening trips to chicken houses where she would help him weigh the birds before they were loaded on the truck.

"When I was younger I would go with my father to the

chicken houses at night and help him catch chickens," Johnelle said. "When Johnnie and I got into the poultry business, I knew a lot more about it than I did about trucking."

A Bunk at the YMCA

Arriving in Little Rock with his borrowed ten dollars, Hunt found a place to stay at the local YMCA. He was assigned a room and the "third bunk from the bottom," lodgings which cost him seven dollars for seven nights. Hunt set out to find a job, motivated by his rapidly depleted finances and his engagement to Johnelle, then attending Arkansas State Teachers College at Conway.

Hunt was hired by East Texas Motor Freight, a trucking firm that based him in Texarkana. For little more than a year, he lived in the company "bunkhouse" and saved his money, eventually putting down a payment on a 1949 Chevy coupe. Johnelle decided to leave college, and in 1952, much to her parents' dismay, she married Hunt and moved to Texarkana.

As the newest driver with the least seniority, Hunt had little choice about his assignments or his schedule. For a salary of forty dollars a week, he had to be available whenever he was called. With no advance notice, he would be assigned brief runs or those requiring several days.

Poor highway conditions added to the challenge, particularly a much-traveled, two-lane highway that crossed national forest land in western Arkansas between Texarkana and Fort Smith. Years later, J. B. Hunt described that 180-mile drive as similar to his boot-camp training during World War II.

"I had the same feeling as when I was crawling underneath barbed wire and live machine gun fire, and after it was over I would brush myself off and say, 'Thank God I made it.' When I got to Texarkana, I would say, 'Thank God I made it.'"[1]

After ten more months in Texarkana, Hunt was transferred to Tuckerman, a town in northeast Arkansas, and the Hunts moved back to Heber Springs.

East Texas Motor Freight shared an Arkansas truck terminal with Superior Forwarding Company, a St. Louis–based carrier. It was at the terminal that Hunt met Superior's board chairman, an outspoken fellow who invited Hunt to drive for his firm. A short time later, Hunt accepted the offer, and in 1953 the Hunts moved to Little Rock. J. B. was assigned a scheduled route to St. Louis that put him on the road for two nights and a day with ten hours at home between each trip.

For the next seven years, the truck driver and his bride maintained a relatively traditional lifestyle. Two children were born, and the Hunts became members of the Gaines Street Baptist Church. The custom of making home visits by church members brought Bob Shell to the Hunts' door one evening in 1955. Shell was invited in, and a lasting friendship developed.

Shell, who went on to establish one of the state's leading construction firms, said the Hunts were regular attendees at church services. J. B. quickly distinguished himself by his trademark white hat and his hearty breakfast appetite following Friday morning prayer meetings, Shell recalled.

Howard Griffen, a poultry-feed salesman who also attended the Gaines Street church at the time, remembered joking with Hunt about his late-night driving.

"One time I asked J. B. how he managed to stay awake all night when he was driving," Griffen said. "He answered, 'I just think about all the people I owe money. I keep slapping my leg and keep on driving.'"

A Truck Driver's Life

For Johnelle, those early years of marriage were the chance to test her own resources. No longer dependent on her parents, she developed the sense of humor and self-reliance that a truck driver's wife requires.

"I always said that whenever he left, the children or the

dog got sick or the plumbing went bad," she said. "I had to learn to take care of all these problems myself. That's part of living with a truck driver."

The mid-1950s also held some important lessons for Hunt. During the years he worked at Superior, Hunt said the chairman rarely stopped in the terminal to chat with his drivers or buy them a cup of coffee. Years later, as chairman of his own firm, Hunt made a point of visiting terminals and talking to the employees, trying, he said, "to do everything Superior didn't do for me when I was working there."

Speaking to his drivers, Hunt sometimes relates a more dramatic episode from his days at Superior. He tells about an argument he had with the company chairman over a policy to use cheaper temporary help when Superior drivers were available for extra work. Hunt said he was back in the terminal with the other drivers when the chairman showed up.

"He walked out and said to all the drivers there, 'I will give anyone here twenty-five dollars to whip this guy.' And he was pointing at me," Hunt said. "I knew I was in the right, and when you're in the right you can do certain things. So I said to the drivers, 'I don't know who you are, but you're going to earn your twenty-five dollars tonight.' They knew I was right, and they didn't bother me."

In addition to truck driving, Hunt was also selling cement, flagstone, and sod as a side business. He stored the sod at his Little Rock home and sold it to nurseries and new home builders in Arkansas. Sometimes he sold it on weekends from Little Rock shopping-center parking lots. Frequently, the energetic Hunt did his own laying of the grass.

"The blood would be running out the end of your fingers from pulling on that grass," he said. "We made money and had a lot of fun."

Some of the sod was purchased through the Winrock Grass Farm, a subsidiary business of Winthrop Rockefeller, who would later be elected governor of Arkansas, and Winrock Enterprises. The Winrock connection was to be extremely valuable for Hunt, but the payoff, still a few years away, would require Hunt's entrepreneurial vision to make it work.

Burning Rice Hulls at Stuttgart

In the late 1950s, Hunt was assigned a new route through eastern Arkansas for Superior Forwarding. The route took him through Stuttgart where he frequently saw rice hulls burning in the fields. The hulls were a processing waste product, and the Stuttgart rice mills paid one dollar a ton to have them hauled away. The piles of burning hulls sent clouds of smoke over the city.

Hunt knew that the hulls had good potential as a base litter for poultry houses, but no economical means of packing or transporting the light, fluffy hulls had yet been devised. Ever since his days in the Heber Springs planer mill, Hunt had been intrigued by the idea of a packing system for poultry litter. He now applied himself to this challenge.

Johnelle recalled him coming in from driving to sit at the table and draw up plans and machine specifications. Another route change at Superior, this one an overnight run from Little Rock to Jonesboro, gave him more time at home each day to plan the rice-hull project.

By 1960, Hunt's project was ready for presentation, but start-up financing, approximately eighty-five thousand dollars, still had to be raised. Hunt knew his part-time sod business could not raise the necessary capital, but he believed he could convince his Winrock business associates to invest in the rice-hull plan.

Hunt called on George Reynolds, Winrock Enterprises' president at the time. Reynolds was not in his Winrock office on Petit Jean Mountain when Hunt arrived, but a secretary, Erma Lela Huett, was astute enough to listen to the truck driver's plans. Hunt, who had never been shy about speaking his mind, apparently impressed her.

"When I told her about the deal, she said 'go back home and don't mention this to anyone. I'll go over this with Mr. Reynolds and he'll call you,'" Hunt said.

In the meetings that followed, a plan was devised for Winrock Enterprises to provide complete start-up financing in exchange for 51 percent controlling interest of the rice-hull operation, Hunt said. The Winrock offer was later modified to an initial investment of $5,533. With Winrock staff drawing up the prospectus for the private stock offering, Hunt was advised to sell as much stock as he could to chicken growers and feed companies.

"During the week they were putting the prospectus together, I took my vacation from Superior. Johnelle and I left Little Rock at midnight and drove up to Springdale," Hunt said. "All the hotel rooms were full, so we slept in the car in front of the Springdale Motel. The next morning when they gave us a room, I took a shower and went out to sell stock."

Hunt said he didn't know any of the poultry growers in northwest Arkansas, but he knew there were many in the area. He visited Tyson Foods, George's Inc., Peterson, and other poultry firms, and his salesmanship skills won the needed investment. Executives at the companies agreed to buy stock in Hunt's new venture and purchase quantities of the rice-hull litter as it was produced.

On August 10, 1961, the first meeting of incorporators and shareholders of The J. B. Hunt Company was held in Little Rock. Reynolds chaired the meeting, and stock price was officially set at one dollar a share. By the end of the month, the *Arkansas Democrat* recorded that ground had been broken at Stuttgart for a one-hundred-thousand-dollar plant that would process and bag rice hulls for poultry litter.[2] When the plant began operation in January 1962, Hunt said it was the only one of its kind in the nation and was expected to dispose of eighty-eight thousand tons of rice hulls annually.[3]

High Risk and Personal Investment

Much was at stake that first year, including a sizable personal investment. The Hunts had sold their Little Rock home and borrowed thirty-five thousand dollars to help finance the plant. Hunt, thirty-four years old with two children, said his biggest risk was leaving a well-paying job for that first entrepreneurial venture.[4]

Now living in Stuttgart, the Hunts both worked in the plant. J. B. kept the packing machines running and drove the truck to deliver hulls. Griffen, who had relocated to Springdale to work for a poultry supply house, told Hunt which poultry growers to call on to sell the litter. Johnelle, who hadn't worked outside the home during her ten years of marriage, assisted with office duties then took on a full-time role as partner to her husband in a business that showed many signs of failure.

"Made me nervous? It scared me to death," Johnelle told the *Arkansas Gazette* in a 1987 retrospective on the Hunts' success. "Everybody said you can't keep operating. Everything we have, everything we ever hope to have is in this. We can't quit. It was a brand new concept, a new product. It took a lot of selling."[5]

Johnelle found her relationship to her husband changed as a result of the new company. She recognized him as the company boss, but she insisted Hunt assure her that his ideas were well founded.

"He's the optimist and has the fantastic ideas and knows it will always work out," she said. "I hold back and ask how. He has to prove to me it will work. Of course if he listened to me, he'd still be driving a truck."[6]

In its first year of operation, The J. B. Hunt Company achieved net sales of $50,626 and a net loss of $19,123. Start-up problems included continual adjustment of the packing machine, a device from an Atlanta engineering firm that Hunt eventually replaced with one of his own design.

Another start-up problem involved the bags used to pack

the rice hulls. The fiber bags had burlap tops sewn in, and each would hold seventy-five pounds of rice hulls. Full bags were delivered to poultry growers, and empties were picked up sometime later. To Larry Behnke, who replaced Reynolds as president of Winrock Enterprises in 1962, the Hunt balance sheets revealed an immediate operational dilemma.

"I saw a tremendous amount of asset in bags, but there were no bags at the plant," Behnke said. "Hunt had a deposit on the bags, but no one was returning them. So we raised the deposit."

In his first report to shareholders, Hunt reported that bag deposits had been doubled to thirty cents to increase returns. The Stuttgart plant was packing twelve hundred bags in an average nine-hour shift, and orders were increasing every day. "We feel certain," Hunt's report stated, "your company should begin to earn a profit, which was a prime motive in the original idea."[7]

A Packing Machine with a "Knock-Down Punch"

The Stuttgart plant began earning a profit by its second year, an achievement Hunt attributes to hard work and luck. Within the next few years, production and profits continued to increase, and bags of rice hulls were being shipped by truck and rail. This rapid success was directly related to the new packing machine Hunt designed. Inspiration for his invention came from boxer Joe Louis and his "knock-down" punch, Hunt said.

"I once heard Joe Louis on the radio explain that from a quarter-inch away, he could not knock a man down," Hunt said. "But at a half-inch, he could do it. What he was really telling me was that you have got to have distance to reflect power. You got to have a little flexibility, no matter how much force you have."

Hunt applied this basic concept to pack rice hulls under pressure. His machine compacted rice hulls inside a metal chute at a four-to-one ratio and stuffed them in a paper sack before they could expand. Had the hulls been given any chance to expand, the relatively weak paper sack would not have been able to contain them.

Hunt's design, in effect, held Joe Louis' punch to the quarter-inch range where it had no knock-down power. The design had been many years in development. Since his early days at the Heber Springs sawmill, Hunt had been working on plans for a poultry-litter packing machine that could fill sacks at maximum pressure. A letter from patent attorneys affirmed that the most important feature of Hunt's new design was the technique in which a paper bag could be loaded with loose material under considerable pressure.[8]

Though consistent use of the new packing machine and the switch from burlap to paper sacks did not occur until the mid 1960s, Hunt had early confidence in his venture. In 1961, after nearly twenty-one years on the road, he quit driving a truck for a full-time role in management.

Through the 1960s, seven of Hunt's packing machines were built and installed in rice-hull mills in Arkansas and other states. Hunt installed the machines at no cost and had the mill personnel operate them. He paid the mill five cents for each filled sack, then he sold the sacks to poultry growers for one dollar each.

"As far as I know, we were the only rice-hull company that never went broke," Hunt said in 1990. Linking his massive trucking firm to the packing machines, he added, "The fortune of this company lies right there in that piece of metal."

A Decision to Sell Out

Shareholders who stayed with the firm would eventually see their initial investment increase by enormous proportions. In 1987, Hunt said that those who put five thousand dollars in chicken-litter stock would be worth twenty-two million dollars.[9] But some initial investors took a short-term position and sold their stock. These included most of the non-poultry-related investors and Winrock Enterprises.

In a 1991 interview, Behnke said his original instructions from Winthrop Rockefeller were "to clean up the balance sheet." In 1962, Winrock Enterprises was in bad financial shape with assets in many small businesses that produced little income, Behnke said.

The Hunt company was a Winrock investment that required a disproportionate amount of management time. Notes from Winrock board meetings mention unresolved production problems and a need for business guidance. Nevertheless, Winrock increased its share holdings in the firm. Behnke was elected chairman of the board of The J. B. Hunt Company in 1962 and he began working closely with Hunt to assist the firm.

With a background in financial analysis, Behnke may have found Hunt lacking in traditional business skills. He recalled a meeting to review truck-leasing papers when Hunt was asked if he wanted to read the documents. Behnke said Hunt, who had been looking out a window during the entire session, declined to review the lease, saying he saw no point in reading it himself if Behnke and the attorney were satisfied with it.

Ed Cromwell, a partner in the Winrock Grass Farm and an original shareholder in the Hunt company, recalled Behnke expressing frustration with the Hunt organization during the 1960s. Behnke was upset because Hunt didn't understand figures and couldn't handle paperwork well, Cromwell said, adding that Behnke once mentioned to him that he doubted the Hunt firm would ever be a success.

Winrock did see potential in the rice-hull firm, but notes from meetings indicate it believed the firm was limited in growth without additional equity financing. So in 1966, Winrock began talking about a merger. Hunt, whose salary that year as rice-hull company president was about ten thousand dollars, would have received a five-year minimum compensation package of nearly twenty-five thousand dollars per year if he brought his company within the Winrock organization. Hunt said he responded with a counter offer, agreeing to the merger if he became new president of Winrock Enterprises. Hunt's proposal may not have been made seriously, but it reflects his bold, personality-based business style. Hunt said he knew Winrock would not accept a "guy who could hardly read or write" as its new president, but he couldn't resist making the offer.

Notes from a 1967 Winrock board meeting offer a more reasonable position. Hunt declined the merger option, the meeting notes indicate, for two reasons: that Winrock was overly concerned with its image in public service and was not a profit-driven organization, and that a merger would disrupt the administrative flow at the rice-hull plant. The notes further state that the Hunt company had achieved its most successful year and the time was not right to push a merger.

Hunt's refusal to give up his majority position in the company forced Winrock to return to its original strategy as a venture-capital operation.

"Once we got a deal going and couldn't help it anymore or couldn't control it, we didn't want to stay on in a minority position," Behnke said. "Had we been given a majority position with Hunt, we would have taken it."

Behnke said another factor contributing to the Winrock decision to sell its Hunt stock was what appeared to be a limited growth potential for the company. In 1968, there was little indication, other than in Hunt's active imagination, of the tremendous expansion that would soon follow.

"We were never that enthused with the company. A poultry litter company, where do you go with that?" Behnke said. "In retrospect, we should have stayed in, but we never looked back."

In November 1968, Behnke proposed a $3.00-per-share buy-back offer. Hunt's counter offer of $2.50 per share was accepted, and Winrock's 18 percent ownership of the company changed hands. The $46,000 buyout gave Winrock a fair profit on its investment. It also returned to Hunt a stock holding that, some twenty years later, would be valued at close to one hundred million dollars.[10]

A year after the stock buy out, Behnke was replaced as Winrock president, a move he said was not related to his involvement with the Hunt business.

Rice Hulls and Much More

By the end of the 1960s, The J. B. Hunt Company was the largest rice-hull dealer in the nation. Sales territory had expanded from Arkansas into Missouri, Iowa, and Illinois, reaching to northern turkey farms in Minnesota and Wisconsin.

Revenue for 1969 was $827,198, and earnings peaked at $51,550. Hunt's first trucking venture was established that year, but the transport division did not begin to dominate corporate activity until the end of the 1970s. It did not earn a profit until some years later.

During the 1970s, the Hunt company invested in a variety of business opportunities, following a strategic course that reflected the enthusiastic energy of its founder. The former lumber salesman and auctioneer became involved in so many business schemes that Johnelle joked about a sign in front of the company, invisible to everyone inside, that said, "Anyone with crazy ideas, stop here. We'll listen."

Some of these ventures involved transporting the rice hulls. Hunt said he designed the first set of double twenty-eight-foot trailers in Arkansas to haul the hulls, but the trailers were so unstable that no one besides himself would drive them. Another trucking misfortune related to the company's first attempts to deliver rice hulls in bulk. A truck with a large bed was fitted with an auger and blower so it could drive down the center of poultry houses and blow in the litter. The process was reasonably successful, but it created a tremendous dust problem.

Hunt was delivering bags of litter to northwest Arkansas

where Paul Maestri, who would later direct the company trucking division, distributed them to local poultry growers. The bags were carried to Springdale in a renovated auto transport truck, a vehicle Hunt purchased in exchange for shares of stock because he hadn't the available cash at the time. Years later, when the value of the stock rose to several hundred thousand dollars, Hunt said it was the most expensive truck he had ever purchased.

Rice hulls as poultry litter had a related value for other livestock bedding, particularly for horse stalls. When horse owners showed little interest in purchasing sacks of litter with pictures of chickens on them, Hunt devised a quick remedy.

"We took the same material and called it horse litter," he said. "We put a picture of a horse on the bag and sold it at fifty cents higher than the chicken litter."

Another venture that turned a quick profit was a wood lathe machine that created large dowel pins. Hunt ran the lathes in the Stuttgart plant for two years. He said his best sale was fifty-five thousand of the large wooden pins to a firm that used them in constructing a tunnel underneath Tokyo Bay in Japan.

A chance meeting at a poultry convention in Pennsylvania gave Hunt distribution rights to an automated egg-gathering system. The Farmer Automation System, which sold for twenty-five thousand dollars, moved hen nests on a long circular conveyer so a poultry farmer could gather the eggs without having to walk the length of his breeder-hen house.

Hunt was impressed by the system, but testing the device back in Arkansas, he learned it would not function with rice hulls. So Hunt began to gain control of buckwheat hulls, a nesting material that worked in the system. "We tied up all the buckwheat hulls in the U.S.," Hunt said. "We made a lot of money at that."

A few misguided investments were made during the 1970s, but none of any large degree. Some of the unsuccessful ventures from the period include a tugboat company at Pine Bluff, a partnership with a Houston firm to sell metal roofing machines, and a water system at Stuttgart. Money was lost on these deals, but some important lessons were learned. "When you invest in a business, you invest in a person," Johnelle said. "Some of the ideas were good, but we invested in the wrong person."

Vitamin Premix and Poultry Supply

The primary activity for The J. B. Hunt Company in the early 1970s was the discovery of a new market for rice hulls. Grinding the hulls allowed them to serve as a base carrier for livestock vitamins and medications. Having no nutritional value of their own, the hulls were an ideal carrier.

At one time, up to twenty hammer mills at the Stuttgart plant were grinding hulls and selling them to pharmaceutical companies such as Eli Lily, Pfizer and Co., and American Cyanamid. Hunt, who for some years had been wanting to relocate to northwest Arkansas, finally realized the opportunity.

In February 1971, plans were announced to construct at Lowell a vitamin premix plant, warehouse, and new corporate office. The company would maintain its Stuttgart plant, but headquarters would move to the new Lowell facility where Hunt would also become a distributor of Pfizer animal health products.[11]

Hunt already had an established warehouse operation at Bentonville where his fledgling truck line, in business since 1969, and his poultry supply division were located. Hunt marketed a variety of poultry products, including transport boxes, feeders and coops, egg cartons, and nesting materials. But in March 1971, a fire destroyed the Bentonville warehouse. The next month, a fire at Stuttgart caused more than four hundred thousand dollars in damages.[12]

The two fires may have slowed Hunt, but they did not stop or dissuade him from pursuing his plans. From Bentonville, Hunt operated out of the neighboring town of Rogers until the Lowell warehouse was completed. At Stuttgart, he arranged a contract with Eli Lily for construction of expanded storage areas.

With financial backing from Pfizer and an agreement to buy their raw vitamins, Hunt began selling a vitamin premix to feed companies from the Lowell warehouse in 1972. Despite a projected market potential, the Lowell premix plant did not become a profit center, although Hunt was able to repay the Pfizer investment over several years by providing ground rice hulls to the company.

The 1970s were a period of mixed fortune for Hunt. While several of his ventures failed, the rice-hull packing machines and grinding mills increased their output and share of corporate profits. Hunt also benefited from support by the board of directors of his privately held corporation. Arkansas-based national poultry leaders such as Gene George and Lloyd Peterson, rice-hull customers for many years, were board members and among the largest shareholders in the firm.

"We had confidence in the company," George said. "Before the public offering of stock, if any of the shareholders wanted to sell, Peterson and I would buy all available shares and split them."

That confidence was shared by board member J. D. Cobb, a farmer and cotton ginner from Keo, Arkansas, who personally bought several acres adjoining the original Lowell site soon after the corporate relocation. George said other board members thought the extra land was not affordable at the time, but Cobb believed the company would soon need the property. In 1974, Cobb sold the land to the company for a minimal profit.[13]

A Trucking Sideline

Hunt's enthusiasm for new business projects brought him many opportunities, but none have succeeded on the scale of the transport division. Like his many other ventures, however, trucking began as a business sideline. It was implemented with limited resources within an environment that offered little opportunity for new and small players. True to form, Hunt began his trucking operation with equipment that others had just about given up on.

In 1969, Hunt was contacted by Red Hudson, a midwest director for Ralston Purina and a large rice-hull customer. Hudson wanted him to meet a Kansas trucking-firm owner named Bill Stephens who hauled dressed poultry out of Arkansas in refrigerated trailers. Stephens wanted to sell out, and Hudson thought the opportunity was perfect for Hunt. With an initial contract from Ralston Purina, Hunt bought five old trucks and seven worn-out refrigerated trailers. He located the trucking division at the Bentonville rice-hull warehouse and began hauling poultry.

The first setback occurred soon afterwards. Ralston Purina withdrew its poultry-processing operations from the area, leaving Hunt with a fleet of "reefers" but no steady customers. Hunt switched to dry van trailers and added more trucks, but industry regulations held back any significant growth.

Since 1935, American trucking had been a regulated industry under the jurisdiction of the powerful Interstate Commerce Commission. The ICC maintained its control until 1980 when the Federal Motor Carrier Act lifted most regulatory barriers and opened the marketplace to free competition. But Hunt's foray into the trucking industry came at a time when new entry was highly discouraged and established carrier-shipper business relations were virtually mandated by federal law.

Under these stringent conditions, Hunt's loss of the Ralston Purina business left him with no ICC allowance to haul anyone else's freight. In 1971, Hunt purchased operating authority from an Atlanta truck firm, the first of many limited-scope relations the transport division would build through the decade. According to the *Arkansas Poultry Times,* the Hunt fleet had grown to thirty-five trucks.[14]

As a new owner of a trucking firm, Hunt had several levels of support that other start-up ventures lacked. With nearly twenty-one years of driving experience, Hunt knew firsthand how trucks and drivers had to operate to survive. More importantly, Hunt had spent the past decade building a successful business and a skilled management team. The trucking venture, as a subsidiary of the rice-hull business, had an established financial base and a board of directors to advise it.

These advantages could barely overcome the tremendous barriers facing a start-up operation in the regulated period. Gene George recalled consistent monthly losses in those early years and Hunt "more than once talking about dropping the truck line."

On the Brink of Deregulation

When Paul Bergant joined Hunt in 1978, the Chicago lawyer was impressed by the firm's aggressive attitude and commitment to growth. Hunt had less than fifty trucks at the time, but it recognized the need for specialized skills to carry it through the deregulation period that lay ahead, Bergant said.

"I was the first specialist they identified to meet their objectives," Bergant, now executive vice president of marketing, said. "They realized the whole regulatory process was an impediment to what they wanted to do, and they needed someone to deal with that."

"I could see this company had the right idea. If anybody could make it in the deregulated environment, they would."

Bergant first worked with Hunt through the Chicago law firm Sullivan Associates where he helped trucking firms untangle the complex legal structure imposed by the ICC. In the preregulation period, competitive rates were never an issue for granting ICC authority. Government approval was contingent on the concept of "public convenience and necessity." Authority for trucking services would only be granted to a new firm if no existing carrier wanted to serve the specific market. Prior to 1980, nearly every request for new ICC authority was opposed by established trucking firms. As a small company, Hunt was able to survive because it picked up limited authority in various exempt products such as poultry and produce, Bergant said. Hunt changed that when it began to file applications in more lucrative, regulated commodities, Bergant added.

"When Hunt made its move, it had to fight major competitors locally and wherever its application might touch in the rest of the country," Bergant said. "The pattern then was to oppose all new entrants, whether they would be a harm to you or not. It was better to stop a small competitor today than have to worry about it later."

Despite the opposition, Hunt began to position itself for a larger market share. In a six-month period ending in November 1975, the company filed forty-five submissions to the ICC. The transport division had six pieces of permanent authority, and a Hunt office had been opened in the Rio Grande valley of Texas.[15] Two years later, authority had been increased to fourteen permanent ICC certificates, with twenty applications on file.[16]

J. B. Hunt's salesmanship skills helped during this slow growth period. He completed negotiations for the purchase of E.L. Reddish Transportation, a contract carrier with ICC authority from Pioneer Foods of Springdale. The acquisition gave Hunt authority to haul to thirty-three states and added two dozen trucks to the corporate fleet. Although ICC approval for the purchase of Reddish was not expected until 1978, by late 1977 Hunt had an interested buyer for the acquired company that would earn him a $230,000 profit.[17]

Early Challenges

When fleet manager Wayne Hensen came to work at Hunt in 1973, he supervised seventy-five drivers who drove trucks so worn out he said it was a challenge to keep them running. When a truck broke down on the road, Hensen called the closest town and got a wrecker out to it.

Many of Hunt's drivers wore long hair and beards despite efforts by highway safety police to inconvenience them with arbitrary road inspections. "Back then, the worse you looked, the more highway safety would bother you," Hensen said. Hunt drivers earned eight cents a mile and did all their own loading and unloading of freight with no additional pay, he added.

Lowell was the only Hunt terminal at the time, and the transport division required consistent underwriting by the rice-hull mills. Hensen, who had sold his bankrupt truck firm in Oklahoma City before joining Hunt, recalled some doubts about the struggling Arkansas truckline.

"I came here broke and I was in better shape than they was," Hensen said. "J. B. always wanted a big trucking company, but there was a lot of times we didn't believe he could do it."

Freight contracts became more available toward the end of the 1970s. The ICC recognized that deregulation was impending, and it began approving nearly all authority applications. By 1978, Hunt reported that 90 percent of its ICC authority requests had been granted, and shipments were being hauled to the west coast.[18]

Wayne Garrison, a former manager of the Stuttgart rice-hull mill, was promoted to chief financial officer and later became corporate president. Garrison had the ability to put ideas to work and get things done. This was a necessary asset and key balance to Hunt's creative vision which sometimes paid little attention to the functional details of a project.

Kirk Thompson, who succeeded Garrison and continues to serve as corporate president, was another key executive who joined the Hunt team in 1973. Thompson's story is illustrative of the strong personal loyalties that were formed in those early years. Originally hired by Johnelle Hunt to work in the all-female accounting department, Thompson was nineteen years old and recently married when he left college to work at minimum wage for Hunt.

Thompson completed his education over the next four years, assisted by the company's first tuition reimbursement plan. Although the Hunts had taken a great personal interest in him and his responsibilities at the company were increasing, Thompson believed his future lay outside of trucking. He decided to take a job with the Arkansas office of the Peat Marwick accounting firm. Before he could leave, however, he had to explain his decision to Mrs. Hunt.

"I refused to take his resignation," Mrs. Hunt said. "We started talking and I started crying and he did, too. He said, 'I feel like I'm telling my mother I'm running away from home.' And I said, 'I feel like I am your mother and you are running away from home.'"

Thompson's resignation was accepted, but J. B. Hunt told him he could always return to the firm. Little more than a year later he did return. Johnelle located him in Texarkana where the young accountant had been sent for a lengthy bank audit that separated him from his wife and second child.

"Mrs. Hunt said she thought it would be a good time to call," Thompson said. "She knew that experience of being separated from your family, and she asked me to come back. I was tired of the traveling. I came back as CFO, the job Wayne had."

Personal relations are an important part of every corporate culture, particularly in a firm's early years when limited size and rapid growth force people to work together in sometimes chaotic conditions.

Hensen recalled the dispatch room in the pre-computer era when all information—drivers' names, trucks, trailers, and assignments—was written on large boards on the walls. Dispatch often continued over the weekend, and Hensen said he had a company WATS line installed in his home to take calls from drivers at all hours.

Ivan Snyder, a regional vice president, spoke of those early days with some nostalgia.

"It was more fun when we were smaller," Snyder said. "We used to have the dispatchers sending out trucks on one side of the room and marketing making the deals on the other. We did a lot of yelling and screaming in the old days, but we got the job done."

2

Deregulation and the Modern Trucking Industry

The American Trucking Associations estimated more than 39,600 trucking firms and 1.5 million tractor-trailer rigs in operation in the United States in 1990. Despite the differences in size and market niche of contemporary motor carriers, one criteria serves as the summary distinction. Trucking firms are primarily recognized as either truckload or less-than-truckload (LTL) carriers. The truckload carrier hauls a single customer's trailer load of freight. The LTL carrier, serving a broader and more fragmented market, fills his trailers with several customers' combined shipments.

Yet the difference between these types relates to far more than freight. Traditionally, the truckload sector has few operating economies of scale, a large number of competitors, and low financial barriers to entry. In contrast, the LTL sector is dominated by a small and still shrinking group of increasingly large national firms and has almost insurmountable financial barriers to entry. Truckload and LTL carriers are so fundamentally different, industry analyst Nicholas Glaskowsky believes the only things the two segments may have in common are that they both operate trucks, carry freight, and use the highway network.[1]

Both truckload and LTL carriers were affected by the 1980 Motor Carrier Act but in dramatically different ways. The truckload sector, now encompassing thousands of small companies, was essentially created by deregulation. The LTL sector, as a result of numerous bankruptcies and acquisitions, has shown a marked decrease in numbers.

The trucking industry transformation which began in 1980 was the first significant change to that market in forty-five years. The Motor Carrier Act of 1935 essentially froze in place the trucking routes at the time. For nearly half a century, the only way to get new route authority was to acquire it from an existing carrier or merge with or acquire another carrier. Regulated carriers hauled both truckload and LTL freight, and rates were subject to strict ICC approval.

This protective environment had been rationalized as a way of guaranteeing service to the public by endowing the trucking industry with a public utilities character. The public was also to be protected from monopoly pricing and destructive competition.

But protection came at a high price. Rate distortions and carrier inefficiency costs in a trucking industry sheltered from competition amounted to several billion dollars annually.[2]

Industry inefficiencies during the regulated period were noted in the following categories:

Routes: Regular-route common carriers had designated routes and could not serve additional areas without new authority from the ICC. New route authority was assigned only if the service was not being provided and would not hurt an existing carrier. Competitive pricing was not considered a relevant factor when applying for new route authority.

Service Authority: Private trucking firms were prevented from acquiring the return loads (backhauls) of other firms' freight.

Commodity Authority: Truckload carriers were generally

small, regional businesses permitted to carry only certain kinds of freight.

Carrier Selection by Shippers: Geographic and commodity restrictions forced shippers, particularly those with dispersed facilities and several product lines, to utilize a number of different carriers.

Rates: Rates for small shipments and for service to thin-traffic communities were subsidized by larger shipments between major transportation centers. Backhaul costs were also passed on to the shipper. A collective-rate bureau system stifled any member's attempt to file rates independently, effectively preventing price competition.

A complex legal process further inhibited change during the preregulation period. The Motor Carriers Lawyers Association protected the interests of authorized trucking firms when new applications were filed at the ICC. The process of legal review could take years, and fees were substantial. The MCLA resisted deregulation when the public initiative began to gain legislative support. Yet the social costs of regulation were perceived as far outweighing the benefits.

Deregulation and New Opportunities

The social awareness for regulatory reform in trucking was matched by similar efforts in the nation's airline and railroad industries. The 1970 bankruptcy of Penn Central, the nation's largest railroad, stirred greater activism and discredited ICC regulatory policies. A 1980 bill deregulating railroads, the Staggers Act, added considerable force to previous regulatory reforms and removed rail rate-setting from ICC review.

"Regulatory reform is a cliché whose time has come," was the 1975 Democratic party policy statement in response to reform initiatives by President Ford.[3] Ford's opinion of the trucking deregulation bill was, "If the teamsters and truckers are opposed to it, it must be a pretty good bill."[4]

Jimmy Carter advanced the reform cause, appointing Alfred Kahn chairman of the Civil Aeronautics Board to deregulate the airline industry. By the late 1970s, deregulation had become a preferred style and a proven winner in the struggle for political policy.

Deregulation showed the capacity of the U.S. political system to transcend narrow interests. It also sent the trucking industry into a shakeout period that has not fully settled. A tremendous number of new business entries followed the 1980 MCA. The bankruptcy rate has increased to more than twelve hundred businesses each year.[5] Many new entrants were underfinanced with little knowledge of how to run a trucking company.

Deregulation took away many functions of the motor-rate bureaus and eliminated exclusive operating franchises. It expanded authority to all areas of the country for new applicants, most of whom were small truckload companies with nonunion employees.

In the LTL sector, carriers lost a large portion of their business to new companies. Many established LTL carriers went bankrupt in the 1980s, while the largest firms, companies such as Roadway and Consolidated Freight, continued to amass a greater market share.

In the truckload sector, the low cost of entry allowed bankrupt companies and equipment to return to use fairly easily. For an LTL carrier, a tremendous capital investment in freight terminals and communication equipment made reentry following a bankruptcy nearly impossible.

Two other factors relating to deregulation became evident in the 1980s. Trucking safety rapidly became a high-profile issue, and a fierce rate war began. Opponents of deregulation can accurately claim that the legislation caused chaos among many companies. But it also allowed a distinctly new type of carrier to emerge, the high-service truckload carrier. This type of company, with J. B. Hunt as its prototype, has most taken advantage of deregulation's open competition.

Surviving the Rate Wars

Survival for a trucking firm in the 1980s meant withstanding the rate discounts the industry was inflicting on itself. Shippers, no longer restricted to one carrier's service or rates, received discounts that undercut published rates by 40 to 50 percent. Big shippers, exploiting the new freedom to negotiate prices, effectively dictated the level of truck rates.

As always, good management was key to survival, as well as the ability to accurately read signals in the market. Some companies recognized deregulation was coming and planned for route expansion. They knew the traffic of their weak competitors would be up for grabs.

Surviving companies were also running a tight ship in cost control. High industry turnover created excess capacity, which further contributed to rate cutting. Uncontrolled rate cutting often degenerated to levels where rates, continually being lowered to gain lost business, no longer covered the cost of doing business.

Larger trucking companies were better positioned against that cycle. They had a strong capital foundation, and they had learned to negotiate rates with shippers and provide the necessary service. Thousands of smaller companies, for either lack of capital base or lack of business skills, could not do the same.

Rate discounting forced austerity measures in many firms, and equipment maintenance became a common area for cutbacks. The rate of truck accidents rose sharply following deregulation, up from 31,500 accidents in 1980 to 39,300 in 1985. The percentage of motor carriers with unsatisfactory safety ratings was highest among new firms and those with the smallest profit margins.[6]

National data on truck safety illustrates the problem. A 1985 survey by the Federal Motor Carrier Safety Assistance Program found 29 percent of inspected trucks insufficiently safe to drive on the highways.[7] In 1986, the *New York Times* reported that 60 percent of trucks inspected in the New York area failed safety tests, the largest problem identified as defective brakes.[8]

In 1987, a *Fortune* magazine article titled "The Scandal of Killer Trucks" stated that large, well-managed companies had maintenance issues under control, but the "vast majority of truckers are a regulator's nightmare." The article further criticized some state efforts in truck accident reporting, quoting an expert from the Center for Auto Safety, a consumer group that monitored truck safety standards, who said some states were doing a "super job" of reporting accidents, but "then you've got others like Arkansas with drool on their chins."[9]

Public concerns about truck safety and the increasing use of triple trailer units have been recently expressed by CRASH, an organization whose suggestive title is an acronym for Citizens for Reliable And Safe Highways. Some trucking leaders believe that funding provided to CRASH by the railroad industry reflects the organization's bias. Others openly challenge the claim that industry safety has deteriorated.

Thomas Donohue, president and chief executive officer of the American Trucking Associations, said in 1990 that double and triple trailer units were the "safest in the country" in accident rates and that general accident and fatality rates for trucking have decreased by 40 percent in the past 10 years in relation to the number of total miles driven.[10]

The federal government has responded to the debate over trucking safety by diminishing the laissez faire policy that accompanied deregulation, authorizing a stricter process for obtaining a Commercial Drivers License, stiffer penalties for safety violations, and more funds for roadside inspection.

For opponents of deregulation, these efforts were too little and too late. The rise of trucking safety violations, they believe, is an unfortunate by-product of the economic imperative of survival in a Darwinian market. Critics of deregulation believe that survival on the brink of bankruptcy, an accepted condition of business for many motor carriers, has created a momentum of deferred maintenance and aged equipment.

Bankruptcy and Industry Consolidation

Price cutting, proper maintenance, and overcapacity are inter-related trucking management problems for which bankruptcy has become a commonplace solution. Supporters of deregulation justify the process for its removal of inefficient carriers from the industry. The large number of carrier bankruptcies in the 1980s reflected the depth of inefficiency that had permeated the industry, deregulation advocates contend.

Trucking business failures actually show a lower rate than that of general businesses, yet a turnover of more than twelve hundred companies a year in any industry creates a legacy of legal and financial problems.[11] In trucking, the residual problem of numerous bankruptcies is being addressed under the auspices of the Filed Rate Doctrine.

Under deregulation, motor carriers were free to establish their own rates, but they were still required to file their interstate tariffs with the ICC. Such a filing made the tariff legally effective.

During the rate wars, many truckers desperate to generate cash flow agreed to new tariffs lower than those previously filed. Many of these new, lower rates were never filed with the ICC. The ICC, for its part, did not enforce the law requiring tariff filing. During the 1980s, the commission's enforcement division held no inspections. To truckers, the indication was that the ICC didn't care if tariffs were filed.[12]

After many companies priced themselves out of business, bankruptcy trustees searching for assets won a legal victory when the Filed Rate Doctrine required unwary shippers to pay the last filed rate even if it was higher than that agreed on with the now-bankrupt carrier.

In 1989, *Traffic World* magazine reported approximately ten thousand undercharge cases in the dockets of the nation's courts. The amount of potential settlement due from shippers was projected at more than two hundred million dollars.[13]

As truckers dropped out of the market, shippers began to realize the liabilities of dealing with low-bid firms and multiple carriers. Shippers also realized that by reducing their selection of carriers, they would reduce transaction costs, maintain smaller transportation staffs, and receive more tailored services.

By 1987, 78 percent of the nation's largest manufacturing firms had reduced the number of carriers they employed, and two-thirds of the group said they expected to further reduce carrier use in the future.[14]

Carrier reduction by shippers gave select trucking firms a larger share of the market. This trend was noted in a survey of trucking-company chairmen who listed continued industry concentration as the single largest change predicted for the 1990s. The chairmen predicted less than five LTL firms would control that industry segment, and a few dozen regional carriers would survive only by servicing their specialized niches.[15]

Critics of deregulation claim this proves that size becomes the survival criteria in an open market, that the big companies get to be bigger still and their small rivals drop into bankruptcy. These critics, however, are overlooking a survival criteria related to size but far more basic.

Quality service is the deciding factor in winning a shipper's business. Size can influence quality because small companies haven't the means to provide computer technology and a nation-wide truck fleet. But shippers build long-term relationships with carriers that provide dependable, high-quality service. The companies that became industry leaders during the rate wars of the 1980s did not diminish their commitment to customer service.

In retrospect, the response to deregulation was relatively predictable. Shippers first took advantage of discounted rates and experimented with new carriers. Then they began cutting back to a core group of the most dependable firms. Thousands of trucking firms priced themselves out of a market they should not have entered in the first place, while a large number of older, established firms found themselves unable to keep abreast of changes in the marketplace.

The truckload sector, with its low entry barriers offering the closest environment for pure competition, should have never been regulated. In the LTL sector, deregulation was a hard blow, a reconciliation with industry inefficiencies that had been around so long many were accepted as routine business.

In response to the surveyed CEOs who expressed surprise at the loss of long-term customer relations, Kirk Thompson offered a concise summary of the post-deregulation period.

"Who would be surprised by customers abandoning long-term relationships?" Thompson speculated. "Only those whose relations had never been tested by economic realities. Welcome to the real world."

Small-Fleet Service

The status of the trucking industry in the early 1990s still reflects the shippers' advantage. Shippers have demanded personalized, small-fleet service from large firms with the critical mass and commitment to become a core carrier. They have also demanded computerized communication, known in the industry as EDI (Electronic Data Interchange) and real-time shipment status reports.

Shippers are getting the trucking services they want, and they have begun to accept the rate increases carriers must charge to provide them. *Transport Topics* wrote that if such shipper fair-mindedness continues, the 1990s would be a much different decade than the 1980s for carrier financial health.[16]

Relatively few truckload firms can provide shippers with the sophisticated services they desire. Clearly, larger firms such as Hunt have the advantage. But along with size, a carrier also needs a defined strategy because, as one trucking industry analyst observed, "the trucker in the future is either going to be a major player or have a carefully defined niche." The truckload sector, another analyst predicted, would go through the same consolidation pressure in the early 1990s as LTL carriers did in the mid 1980s.[17]

Truckload carriers, however, must do what the LTL sector failed to do a decade earlier. The successful truckload company must dramatically change its business practices. Three areas where changes are currently being made are types of drivers, state registration, and driver retention efforts.

A primary aspect of change will be the rejection of single driver owner-operators, a mainstay of traditional truckload operations, in favor of nonunion driver teams and relays. This change in driver usage keeps tractors operating more hours each day and lets advanced truckload companies concentrate on high-density traffic corridors with balanced freight flow. High vehicle use and lower costs are the result.

Independent operators are not an endangered species. Many opportunities remain because a large number of smaller trucking firms rely on independents to take up slack in operations. And nearly 94 percent of the entire trucking industry is composed of these small Class III carriers with annual gross revenues of less than one million dollars. But the advanced truckload firms, those the analysts call "high service" firms, are using fewer owner-operators.

Another factor of change for truckload carriers in the 1990s will be the basic cost efficiency of registering vehicles in a state with relatively low highway user fees. Arkansas, ranked thirteenth in the nation for total annual fees, offers little enticement for truck companies to register their vehicles. In contrast, Oklahoma, where Hunt trucks are registered, is ranked forty-first in the nation for highway user fees Bruce Jones, Hunt chief financial officer from 1986 through 1991, rates the Oklahoma environment for trucking "one of the best in the nation" because of low taxes and an administrative willingness to work with new trucking firms.

Explaining why his trucks were registered in Nebraska, Dean Cannon, head of the Springdale-based Cannon Express Trucking, said, "You can't afford the luxury of being registered in Arkansas."[18]

Finally, advanced truckload carriers will make a concerted effort to decrease the high rate of driver turnover. Driver turnover rates of 100 percent and higher for new drivers are not uncommon. Some truckload companies operate their own training schools and maintain full-time driver training teams. Hunt's national network of terminals is an attempt to recruit and base drivers in areas near their homes, thereby decreasing job dissatisfaction of being away from home for long periods. Incentives are also offered to recruit experienced drivers away from better-paying, short-haul LTL jobs.

But the industry expansion continues to offer tremendous job selection for drivers. For those with good records, opportunities abound to move from one trucking firm to the next, and driver turnover rates are expected to remain high.

The contemporary trucking industry is in a state of flux. In the truckload sector, the hopes of deregulation have been reached, and, despite low profit margins, no decrease of competition is projected. In its annual industry trend issue, *Transport Topics* predicted that trucking will "continue to be dominated by growing costs, increased competition, mergers, bankruptcies, stable levels of ton-miles, and heightened demands from shippers." The magazine further predicted new traffic from the large private carriage market and from railroads.[19]

Yet many railroad and trucking firms are maintaining their fiercely competitive attitudes. And deregulation critics still insist that the only winners have been large carriers and shippers, with small businesses, small towns, and rural communities being the heaviest losers.

Twelve years after it began, the industry turmoil caused by deregulation seems far from over.

A three-year-old J. B. Hunt (left) with his brothers, Leon (middle) and O. D. (right).

The DeBusk family, mid-1940s. Back row, from left: Gloria, David, Johnelle. Front row: Ollie, Dennis, Johnie.

J. B. Hunt, army private, 1945.

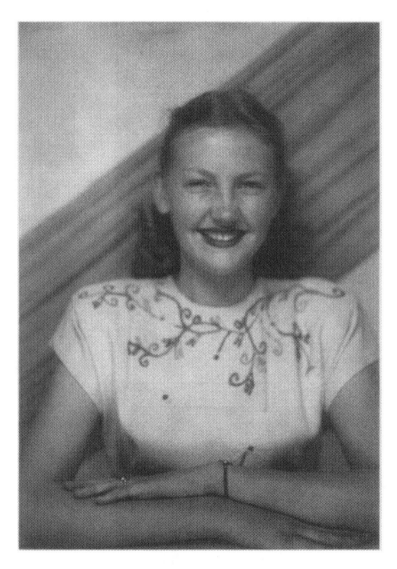

Johnelle DeBusk, sixteen years old.

Seventeen-year-old J. B. Hunt (left) with other workers from the Heber Springs sawmill, 1944.

The Hunt wedding party, 1952, included Johnelle's sister, Gloria, and J. B.'s cousin, Sumler Hunt, his partner in the Heber Springs livestock auction business.

Rice-hull delivery truck at the Stuttgart plant, 1960s, prior to the use of the paper-sacking machines.

Packing machine at the rice-hull plant when burlap sacks were still being used, 1964.

Logo from The J. B. Hunt Company.

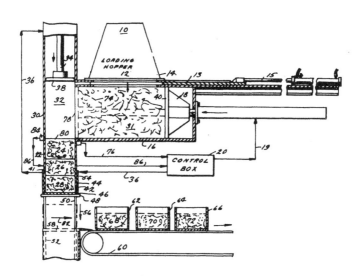

Drawing submitted to the U.S. Patent Office for the rice-hull packing machine designed by J. B. Hunt.

The April 1971 fire at the Stuttgart rice-hull plant caused more than four hundred thousand dollars in damages. A month earlier, a fire destroyed Hunt's newly established poultry supply warehouse in Bentonville.

A Hunt delivery truck loaded for departure from the Stuttgart plant, mid-1970s. Hunt's technique for pressure-packing paper bags of rice hulls made transporting the material economically feasible.

Board of directors for The J. B. Hunt Company. Seated left to right: Roy Grimsley, Tyson's Foods, Springdale, Arkansas; J. D. Cobb, Cobb Brothers, Keo, Arkansas; Paul Vaughn, Valmac, Inc., Little Rock, Arkansas; and Gene George, George's Feed and Supply, Springdale, Arkansas. Standing left to right: Kirk Hale, Peterson Industries, Decatur, Arkansas; Dr. Clifford Treat, White Oak Enterprises, Inc., Camden, Arkansas; David DeBusk, Red River Feed Company, Heber Springs, Arkansas; Johnnie Hunt, The J. B. Hunt Company, Stuttgart, Arkansas. Not present: Fred Darragh, Darragh Company, Little Rock, Arkansas.

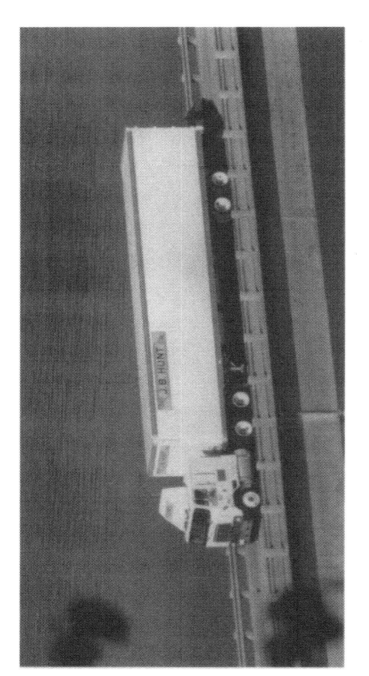

Hunt's fifty-three-foot trailers are a common sight on the nation's highways.

The Hunt terminal at Lowell maintains a large inventory of parts for full tractor service and is one of several hub terminals where complete engine overhaul or replacement can be performed.

Kirk Thompson, president and chief executive officer.

Driver supervisors maintain contact with drivers and assign freight loads. Hunt's computer systems monitor and analyze transport performance.

Tire repair and other routine maintenance is provided at all Hunt terminals.

Under the Quantum intermodal partnership with Santa Fe railroad, Hunt trailers are frequently hauled on flatcars.

The driver training school at Lowell provides a week of classes to all new drivers. An additional three weeks of classes are provided at each new driver's home terminal.

A cooperative agreement with the Mexican carrier Fletes Sotelo established Hunt de Mexico, the company's first international partnership.

J. B. and Johnelle Hunt.

Bryan Hunt, vice chairman of the board.

A white Stetson hat has long been standard attire for the corporate chairman.

Hunt flatbed trailers allow regional transport of containerized cargo from railroad and ship yards.

3

Corporate History Since 1980

When deregulation restructured the trucking industry, Hunt had two distinct advantages over the thousands of other motor carriers granted new operating authority by the ICC.

The Stuttgart rice-hull operation had significantly expanded, and new markets in vitamin premix had been developed with the installation of grinding equipment. Corporate revenue of $25.2 million in 1980 had increased by 72 percent over 1979, following a 45 percent revenue increase over 1978. Wayne Garrison and Kirk Thompson, both twenty-seven years old in 1980, were leading a management team that had gained valuable experience in an environment of extraordinary corporate growth.

The company's second advantage coming into the 1980s was J. B. Hunt's familiarity with the daily operations of trucking. Though Hunt did not personally manage the transport division, his years as a driver had left him with keen insight toward successful practices. As the company's most experienced player, J. B. Hunt became its most proficient coach.

The combination of a skilled management team and a seasoned leader was a great asset. Hunt could make the right choices for the firm, and his young, energetic staff could make them happen. This strategic balance was made even more effective by a distinct lack of similar expertise at all but a handful of other trucking firms.

While the Hunt team was refining its corporate skills, the majority of other trucking firms were doing a dismal job. In its 1981 annual report, Hunt stated that national trucking-company sales had decreased by 7 percent and profits were down by 17 percent from the previous year. According to the report, sixty of the eighty-five carriers with revenue between twenty and thirty million dollars showed a poorer operating ratio than Hunt. Average operating ratio for the industry in 1980 was 96.32. For Hunt, it was 92.6.

The ICC granted Hunt general commodity authority for the forty-eight states at the same time it allowed free market forces to work. "All this came together in 1981 and 1982," Thompson said. "The company really turned around, and before you knew it, we were the industry leader in profitability."

The Hunt 1982 annual report said that despite external pressures of decreasing freight rates and high interest rates, the past year had been the corporation's most profitable. Freight revenue accounted for 92 percent of total business.

In his letter to shareholders, J. B. Hunt articulated the corporate goal and optimism that motivated the firm during the years.

"We are dedicated to making our company an industry leader in all aspects. In 1981, we feel we established a trend toward a new era of growth and profitability that will ultimately result in our reaching that objective. The vast potential of our still young company has only begun to be tapped."

By 1982, Hunt was rated one-hundred-twenty-ninth largest carrier in the nation. Corporate personnel had increased to nearly 650 people, and an employee profit-sharing plan had been established. In those days, J. B. Hunt would greet all employees as he walked through the Lowell offices, and employee parties were held at the Hunts' Springdale home.

With his increasing corporate success, Hunt found time

had become available to cultivate his first non-work-related pastime, described by Johnelle in a 1981 letter:

"After our 30 years of marriage and no hobbies, only work, Johnnie and I got horses, bought 35 acres right behind our house, and are enjoying life to the fullest. We ride after work and on weekends. Johnnie shows in horse shows (gaited horses where they wear tux and all). He also rides in rodeo parades. Last week we had the Rodeo of the Ozarks and he rode in two parades and the grand entry at the rodeo all four nights."[1]

The Low-Cost Producer

Having established an early lead over most other companies in the deregulated trucking industry, Hunt's operational policies further distanced it from the crowd. By converting its fleet to all company-owned and employee-operated vehicles, Hunt had a standardization edge in operations, parts, and service. Hunt's average miles per gallon and total miles per tractor exceeded industry averages, as did the company percentage of new trucks in the total fleet.

John Larkin, an investor analyst specializing in transportation at Alex Brown and Sons, said all these factors contributed to Hunt's becoming the industry low-cost producer.

"Hunt decided that while owner-operators were having an impact, the way to really come at the market was to buy your own trucks and manage your own drivers," Larkin said. "That gave him rate flexibility and a low-cost position. He played that strategy brilliantly through the 1980s."

For Thompson, the corporate strategy was not necessarily unique. The company just did a good job of executing it, he said. Hunt added professional management and increased operational discipline to complement the strategic use of company drivers and equipment, Thompson said.

Garrison, who became company president in 1982, has been credited with establishing the company's strong, centralized leadership and focus on equipment utilization. It was a time when, according to Hunt's son Bryan, the "last thing we needed was an expert." What the company did need was a demanding executive whose single focus could hold together an increasingly complex and diverse enterprise.

Garrison's corporate work ethic balanced Hunt's more amiable leadership. In the corporate world, this is a less popular but equally necessary role, particularly when a firm is experiencing tremendous growth. And in 1983, Hunt was in a growth explosion.

Personnel had increased to 1,050 people, including 787 drivers. Equipment totals were 550 tractors and 1,049 trailers, and an order had been placed for 150 new International Harvester tractors, each priced at approximately seventy thousand dollars. Corporate revenue had increased by 56 percent to sixty-three million dollars, and earnings were up by 142 percent over 1982. A two-for-one stock split added to the financial gains of private shareholders.

Further strengthening Hunt's market position was the company's posture during a nationwide strike by independent truckers. For eleven days in February 1983, truckers protested new taxes on oil, fuel, tires, and heavy vehicles that were included in the Surface Transportation Assistance Act of 1982. Hunt drivers operated continuously through the strike, certainly adding to the antagonism they received from truckers of less successful firms. But the loyalty of Hunt drivers likely impressed shippers who were starting to cut back on the number of motor carriers they contracted.

An Initial Public Offering

By the fall of 1983, a public offering of stock was agreed on by the board of directors. The stock offering would provide new capital to offset corporate debt and would create a sufficiently large amount of shares for individuals to accumulate significant holdings.

J. D. Simpson of Stephens, Inc., the Little Rock securities firm, recalled Garrison contacting him to ask if Stephens was interested in underwriting the initial public offering. With strong positive impressions of the firm, Stephens joined Alex Brown and Sons in coordinating the Hunt stock offering.

"There were five or six other truckload companies going public that year, but Hunt was the Cadillac of those," Simpson said. "We had never done an IPO for a trucking firm before, but it was a business as well run as any we'd seen. Never mind that it was a truck company. It was a growth company. We priced Hunt aggressively and put our money in there, too."

Simpson mentioned Hunt's 30 to 45 percent annual fleet expansion and the lowest operating ratio in the nation among large trucking firms. He was also impressed that Johnelle Hunt was deeply involved in the company through her role in accounts receivable.[2]

Simpson's advice was to simplify corporate transactions by selling the rice-hull mill, an idea previously brought up at Hunt management meetings. The rice-hull business, though still profitable, had limited growth potential, and with corporate headquarters at Lowell, the Stuttgart location added a travel burden to division management.

In September, the rice-hull operation was sold for $2.4 million to the Eli Lilly company, one of Hunt's largest customers for ground hulls. Two months later, corporate stock split at 5.8 to 1 and a public offering sold 1.6 million shares, generating another $18.5 million. Hunt completed the milestone year essentially debt free.

In a preliminary prospectus to the stock offering, Hunt identified three customer types in its target market: high-volume shippers seeking a dependable source of service; shippers shifting from private to common carriers; and former LTL customers whose consolidated freight was now more suited to truckload business. These ideal customers

formed a "service sensitive" segment of the truckload industry for whom Hunt would provide "premium service and
charge compensatory rates" rather than compete primarily
on the basis of price.

This strategic approach to corporate marketing was
designed by a sophisticated executive team. For J. B. Hunt,
however, personal success had not been accompanied by formal changes. Bob Shell recalled a shareholders' meeting at
Lowell prior to the public offering when each person in the
group offered brief remarks and congratulations. Shell said
his comment, meant as a joke, was that success hadn't
changed J. B. because his grammar was as bad as it had always
been.

"I called the next day, thinking that he might have taken
my remark as a put down," Shell said. "Johnelle told me that
J. B. was so proud of my remark he had been telling all his
friends about it."

Above-Average Growth

Through the mid-1980s, Hunt continued to lead the
industry in operating ratio. The company's efficiency factor,
shown below in comparison to the industry average, was a
major factor in its dynamic growth through the decade.

Operating Ratio

	1983	1984	1985	1986	1987
J. B. Hunt	78.6	75.4	79.6	77.1	85.0
Trucking Industry	95.9	96.19	96.49	95.04	96.97

Source: American Trucking Associations and J. B. Hunt records

The achievement was recognized by a *Business Week* ranking as fourth in the nation among the "Best Little Growth
Companies in America."[3] An Equitable Securities research
report cited Hunt's top industry position in operating ratio

and said the company was well positioned for the "virtually untapped sixty billion dollar private carriage truckload market."[4]

Hunt also earned an "Above Average" opinion on a Merrill Lynch research report that reviewed company efforts to deal with industry-wide driver shortages. When the corporate fleet first exceeded one thousand tractors in 1985, a decrease was noted in the driver-to-tractor ratio and in equipment utilization, evidenced by fewer miles driven per tractor per month. With the opening of four new terminals, all performance factors increased, the report stated.[5]

Hunt's new terminals in North Little Rock and at locations in California, Ohio, and New Jersey gave the company a more prominent national presence and greatly boosted driver recruiting efforts. The driver terminal program was so successful that by the end of the decade nineteen Hunt terminals would be located in high-traffic areas across the nation.

J. B. Hunt, commenting on company incentives for fuel economy, said his drivers were limited to fifty-five miles per hour on the highway but they stepped briskly when in the terminals. "All we got is fast walkers," Hunt said. Referring to corporate growth, he added, "It seems like the harder we work, the luckier we get."[6]

More than luck was required for Hunt to grow to its 1986 position as the nation's third largest irregular route truckload carrier or to be ranked 31st by *Forbes* magazine among the "200 Best Small Companies in the U.S."[7] A simple explanation was offered in the 1986 annual report video. High revenue plus low operating costs equaled climbing profits, the video stated.

But there was more going on at Hunt than could be captured in a summary video presentation. A secure management structure was in place, evidenced by the January 1986 announcement that Thompson was replacing Garrison as corporate president. Garrison accepted a less demanding position as vice chairman of the board, giving up all daily involvement with the company. His fortune well established in stock holdings, the thirty-five-year-old retiree moved to Kentucky to pursue a new involvement in horse farming.

Garrison declined to comment about his years of activity with Hunt or his decision to step down from a pivotal role. In the larger context of corporate development, however, his departure can be understood as a transitional phase between two distinct management styles.

Garrison's skill in strong, centralized leadership was a valuable resource for keeping a team on task. But as a corporate team matures, it faces more complex decisions and a larger scope of issues to be resolved. In this phase of growth, delegation of responsibility and participatory management is key to success.

"Garrison was a very good executor of J. B. Hunt's strategic vision," John Larkin observed. "He took the company to one hundred million dollars, then gave it to Kirk Thompson, who has become a strategic thinker. Most companies don't do that. They hold onto the operations guy too long before switching over to the management guy."

Bryan Hunt agreed with that assessment, but he recalled being puzzled when first learning of Garrison's plans.

"It took me years to realize that Wayne probably had a secret agenda," Bryan Hunt said. "He knew where the company needed to be on a certain date, and he got us there, but part of that agenda was that on the next day he wasn't going to be there. That's a rare quality. People always ride the horse one lap too far."

For Thompson, the transition was well planned and smoothly implemented. A two-for-one stock split was announced in May 1986, and for the fourth year in a row Hunt had the best operating ratio in the truckload industry. Progress in operations included installation of a voice messaging system at Lowell to better respond to thousands of daily phone calls and a computer EDI system to speed data exchange with customers.

The foundation for these accomplishments was developed during Garrison's tenure at the company, and it is to his credit that the teamwork necessary to achieve them could assume control without a noticeable slippage. One of the more subtle measures of leadership is how well one's successors continue in your absence.

An Announcement of Goals

Never one to look back, J. B. Hunt used a speaking engagement in Little Rock in December 1986 to announce his latest corporate goals. One objective was to install mobile telephones in all trucks to help drivers maintain better family contact and to better track fleet movement and head off trouble.[8] The telephone plan was later replaced by more sophisticated computer and satellite systems for in-route communication.

Hunt's second corporate goal was to achieve one billion dollars in annual revenue by 1992, almost five times the current-year total. Hunt said the financial goal might be achieved sooner than 1992 if the company could beat its 35 percent annual growth rate and sustain the 50 percent level expected for 1986.

Growth of this type can burn out an executive, and trucking-company presidents tend to burn out every five years, Hunt said. But after twenty-five years in trucking, Hunt claimed he was unaffected by such pressure because "I'm cheering. I'm not carrying the ball."

Earlier in 1986, the fifty-nine-year-old Hunt had hinted at his corporate longevity with a remark about making "millionaires of one hundred employees before I turn 75."[9]

A "Closely Watched" Company

By 1987, Hunt's efficiency efforts began to earn the company a new status in the financial community that studied trucking.

The *Arkansas Gazette,* quoting an analysis report from the

Morgan Keegan securities firm, wrote that Hunt was the most profitable major trucking company in the country and "was closely watched by other companies in the industry for changes in strategy or equipment." [10]

Security analysts at Value Line predicted Hunt revenue would rise by 40 percent to $275 million. Thompson, seeking to downplay the increasing speculation about the company, suggested a 30 percent increase in 1987 revenue.[11] As it turned out, both predictions were wrong. Hunt revenues increased to $286 million that year, a 41 percent rise over 1986.

In the July issue of *OTC Review*, Hunt was rated 46th among the "100 Fastest Growing NASDAQ Companies."[12] Two months later, the magazine ranked Hunt 110th among the top 500 over-the-counter stocks.[13] And *Forbes* magazine bestowed on J. B. Hunt its elite distinction, ranking him 365th on its annual list of the 400 richest Americans.[14]

Hunt had broken new ground with its switch to company vehicles and employee drivers. Responding to an increased demand for drivers and freight, Hunt ordered 1,100 new Navistar International tractors in 1987. In addition to the maintenance savings from standardized equipment, Hunt drivers were provided incentives for fuel economy, and truck engine performance was recorded and analyzed by the in-cab Trip Master computers.

When the national highway speed limit was increased to sixty-five miles per hour, Hunt drivers were instructed to maintain a fifty-five-mile-per-hour limit. Trucks operating at higher speed were less fuel efficient, which raised costs across the industry. Hunt drivers saved the company approximately four million dollars a year in fuel costs by keeping to the lower speed.[15]

Hunt's network of truck terminals was increased with the opening of seven new facilities. Construction of major hub terminals for full vehicle maintenance work was completed at Lowell and in three other states. The new and expanded terminals served the company well in a year when the demand for more drivers was accelerated by a healthy economy and improving overall carrier returns.

With its computer system upgraded to a new IBM mainframe system, Hunt could more rapidly respond to customer inquiries and communicate more efficiently across its growing terminal network. New marketing territories were established, and the external sales forces doubled in size. Service to Canada was begun, and a new automotive department was established to better respond to time-sensitive shipments for the auto industry.

J. B. Hunt saw no reason to curb his optimism about the future. He announced at the April shareholders' meeting that the revenue goal of one billion dollars, previously set for 1992, was being reset for 1991. Hunt gave specific details of his year-end and five-year predictions. Fleet size would increase from 2,600 to 8,300 tractors and total number of employees would rise from 5,700 to 16,000 by 1991, he said. The corporate phone bill, approximately twenty-seven thousand dollars per day in 1987, would triple in five years, Hunt predicted.[16]

In the 1987 annual report video, future promise was presented as an achievable goal because Hunt currently had less than 1 percent of a sixty-billion-dollar potential market. Two-thirds of all freight was carried by private companies who would achieve better economy by hiring Hunt than maintaining their own trucking fleets, the video stated.

J. B. Hunt concluded the video with his personal touch of confidence. "We've passed the roadblock of driver shortage," he said. "We passed the curve and now we're ahead of the pack."

An Unchallenged Position

With its pattern of growth well established, Hunt approached the end of the decade with an unchallenged position in the industry. Revenue for 1988 was more than $392 million. The $106.1 million one-year increase over 1987 represented the total size of most of the firm's competitors. J. B. Hunt, repeating his prediction of one billion dollars in revenue, shifted that achievement back to 1992, but added, "We'll have to slow up to do that."[17]

With a 30 to 50 percent annual growth since 1983, Hunt seemed well deserving of the continued recognition directed at the company. Thompson was included on *Business Week*'s "corporate elite," a list of chief executive officers from the nation's largest companies. In its capsule summary of the company and its leadership, the magazine wrote that "Hunt added docks and bays faster than it booked new business, and the company was hurt by the shortage of qualified drivers. Low keyed and studious, he [Thompson] solved the problems. Now he's asking for higher prices—and getting them."[18]

Even the Hunt corporate communications department was setting national standards. *Financial World* magazine awarded first prize to the department for its production of the 1988 annual report video, a colorful and patriotic tour of American landscapes with Hunt drivers describing their jobs.

By the end of the year, nine new terminals had been added, bringing the total to sixteen. Six hundred new trucks raised the corporate fleet size to 3,135 vehicles, the largest fleet dedicated to truckload shipping by a publicly held company. Second largest in that segment was Builders Transport with 2,200 trucks.

New services into Mexico and Canada were supported by increased personnel in the marketing department. To meet a continuing demand for qualified drivers, Hunt established a driver training school at Lowell. The school, another industry milestone, offered no-cost training and a guaranteed job to graduates. In the first year, Hunt driver turnover across the company decreased by 5 percent.

A portion of the new drivers were probably from Arkansas,

giving added reason for the Arkansas department of the American Legion to recognize Hunt with its Employer of the Year Award for hiring nearly four hundred veterans. J. B. and Johnelle continued to share their good fortune with a variety of private donations. In late 1988, state newspapers mentioned two of these: a cellular phone system donated to the tiny Lowell Fire Department, and the creation of a meditation chapel at the Arkansas Cancer Research Center in Little Rock.

The End of a Decade

By the end of 1988, Hunt was still the analysts' favorite trucking stock. Andras Petery of Morgan Stanley predicted Hunt would "continue to dominate the nonunion truckload industry" and would soon pass its primary competitor, Schneider Truck Lines.[19] Ginanne Long of Stephens said she expected the price of Hunt stock, then at $22.75 per share, to rise to $33 within a year.[20] And *Business Month* magazine listed the firm as thirty-seventh among the nation's two hundred fastest growing public companies in the last five years.[21]

Fourth quarter earnings of $8.5 million, a stunning 77.7 percent increase over 1987, seemed to indicate the Arkansas truckline would make good on every forecast of growth. But the inevitable news came with first quarter 1989 projections. Hunt cut its estimated growth earnings, and blaming bad weather, higher fuel prices, and extra driver pay, the company said it was expecting flat or decreased profits for the period.[22]

The truckload industry in 1989 had forced prices downward because of overcapacity, a prolonged rise in fuel prices, and an uncertain economy. Hunt adjusted its growth plans accordingly, cutting back purchases from 1,600 tractor-trailers to 900 and decreasing its projected driver needs from 1,850 to 1,000.

"By doing this," Thompson told shareholders at the annual meeting, "we are sending a clear message that we do not intend to force growth that is not there. We are not initiating nor do we intend to participate in a rate war to obtain a market share."[23]

J. B. Hunt told shareholders that "one little bad quarter" wasn't going to scare him. He said he was not going to apologize for the soft quarter because "a lot of people didn't make anything at all, and if they had made what we did they'd have thought they'd got rich."[24]

Hunt's point was that success is a relative value. The 30 percent revenue increase in 1989 was the company's smallest percentage increase since 1981. Earnings also reversed an upward trend begun nine years earlier. Yet Hunt's 30 percent growth was among the ten best for common carriers, and its operating ratio of 87.9 was the lowest among that group.

Midway through the year, John Larkin said, "We still think on a long term basis the company is the truckload leader and will probably get back on track with up earnings next year provided the economy lands softly as most people are predicting. Hunt is a bell wether company. They have a positive future ahead of them."[25]

Hunt accomplished a great deal in 1989. A logistics department was created to match loads to available drivers for better use of equipment and on-time service. New fifty-three-foot trailers were introduced, new terminals were opened in St. Louis and Detroit, and new driver recruitment strategies filled trucks in the midst of industry shortages.

Late in 1989, a partnership between Hunt and the Santa Fe Railroad created Quantum, an intermodal service that linked rail and truck services for efficient freight transport between west coast and midwest cities. The Quantum partnership, discussed in more detail in chapter seven, was a strategic move for Hunt at this time. The joint venture could be a "six-hundred-million-dollar deal," J. B. Hunt said. Its more immediate benefit, he implied, was in reflecting the corporate position as a major player in the transportation industry.

"We're doing a couple of joint ventures with some other people beside the railroad, and this is something I'm really proud of," Hunt said. "At least we're visible enough to know that other people are watching us and we're watching other people."[26]

Hunt also began construction of a new headquarters facility at Lowell. Yet despite these accomplishments, 1989 signaled a slowdown to the growth which the company had experienced since 1980. Even by the end of the year, when market forces had turned around to the point that shippers were willing to discuss and accept price increases, Hunt had a different understanding of the strong demand for its trucking services.

"The issue is not demand, but margins on that demand," Thompson wrote in the annual report. The statement implies that Hunt would have to become more innovative in all affairs. With shippers accepting higher rates, excellent customer service would become an assumed standard, something carriers would have to provide simply to stay in business. Future profits, Thompson's remark suggests, would depend on service innovations and how much time and effort it would cost to provide them.

A Period of Mixed Blessings

At the start of 1990, Hunt had entered a period of mixed blessings. The company was recognized as the largest truckload carrier in the nation in reports published by *Distribution* and *Transport Topics* magazines.[27] In April, *Business Week* ranked Hunt 823rd in "America's 1,000 Most Valuable Companies," and in May, *Business Month* listed the firm as 50th fastest growing among the nation's top 100 companies.

The company's continuing dominance was also acknowledged by *Forbes* magazine who wrote that Hunt's 40.4 percent average five-year growth was comparable to the 7.9 percent of other trucking firms and 11.3 percent for the entire transportation industry.[28]

The down side of these accolades was that Hunt's $509.2

million revenue for 1989 was the lowest percentage increase the company had seen in eight years. Profits had decreased by 7 percent to $30.6 million, the first time in the deregulation period that Hunt earnings had failed to exceed those of the preceeding year.

Despite the addition of seven hundred trucks, the demand for company services had exceeded the level of the previous year. The company was doing more business than ever before, yet it was making less money. Its operating ratio, though still significantly below the industry average, had also increased.

Rising costs and flat-to-decreasing freight rates were the problem. *Transport Topics* wrote that 1989 was a year "most trucking executives were glad to see end. The same goes for the 1980s as a whole." A decade that began with deregulation and a recession ended with some of the worst financial performances in the industry's history, and "in between came crisis after crisis: insurance, interest rates, fuel prices, driver shortages, rate wars, and more," the magazine wrote.[29]

Yet some analysts had the insight to look beyond the surface indicators. The conclusions they drew about Hunt were far more promising than the summary explanation of industry woes. Richard Holt of Prudential Bache said "the bottom line in this case is what you see is not necessarily what you get." The decline in earnings reflected an aggressive expansion program and an increased debt burden to grow the fleet. These long-term investments were already being offset by improved productivity in equipment and personnel, Holt said.[30]

Hunt executives were "obviously not pleased" with the financial results for the year, the 1989 annual report stated. At the shareholders' meeting in May, several of them explained what the company was planning to do about it.[31]

Concerned with volatility in earnings, Bruce Jones, Hunt chief financial officer, said the company would "break with the successful strategy of 'grow, grow, grow' predominant in the 1980s" and focus instead on a long-term strategy of smaller capital expenditures and a 15 percent annual increase in revenue and earnings. "The idea is to build strength while looking for innovative ways to grow and effectively reduce overall industry capacity," Jones said.

Thompson also touched on the capacity issue, stating that current demand for additional capacity had to be considered in light of driver availability and adequate rate relief. "For the long-term good, it may be better to forgo adding additional equipment this year," Thompson concluded.

But it was J. B. Hunt who characteristically brought the complex issues into layman's terms. Major corporate customers were studying the firm because of its success. But the company is only "half as smart as they think we are," Hunt said.

"If we can slow up and get in the position that everybody thinks we are, we're going to get filthy rich," Hunt said. "We're acting now like we're in Chapter 11. We're doing a lot of cutting all over."

A "Lousy Year" for Truckload

Ginanne Long summed up the mood of many trucking analysts in her comments in a Stephens research report. "It's been a lousy year for the truckload industry, and it doesn't seem to be getting any better," Long wrote, but she noted that Hunt had been busy strategizing for the future. The company had made several moves to better position itself for the 1990s.[32]

The driver-shortage issue had been a concern since the mid-1980s. Hunt had previously responded with a guaranteed minimum salary for drivers, the opening of its driver training school, and a good management focus on meeting overall driver needs.

But industry-wide driver shortages returned as a 1990 issue, caused in part by a shrinking work force, by curtailment of government-sponsored loans for trade-school students, and by experienced drivers leaving the profession. To attract more experienced drivers, Hunt raised its pay scale for new hires and returned to a per-mile pay basis for all drivers. Hunt's top rate of thirty-three cents per mile for drivers with four years' experience was the highest in the truckload industry, the company said.

The oversupply of used equipment was a problem less easily addressed by internal adjustments. In the 1980s, Hunt had been able to secure an equitable trade on its tractors and maintain a relatively new fleet. But in 1990, a decreasing value for used tractors reduced that advantage.

Thompson illustrated the changing depreciation rate of used trucks in the corporate newsletter. A $50,000 three-year-old truck was worth $33,875 in 1986, but a truck of equal value and age was only worth $28,260 in 1990. Lower trade values meant older equipment was kept in service longer despite higher maintenance costs and loss of efficiency in long-haul lanes, Thompson wrote.[33]

The corporate response to the used equipment problem was typically bold and unpredicted. In October 1990, Hunt announced it was expanding operations into the flatbed and short-haul truckload business with the acquisition of Bulldog Trucking, a regional short-haul van and flatbed carrier in Carnesville, Georgia. Hunt also announced it would create a new corporate flatbed division with national scope that would operate out of Hueytown, Alabama. Short-haul service was further enhanced with a Hunt presence in the Chicago and New York City metropolitan areas.

Flatbed trucking, with a large freight market in construction materials, is primarily a short-haul operation. Hunt's assignment of two hundred tractors to the new division, in addition to Bulldog's five hundred trucks, offered a highly practical solution to the problem of used equipment. Projected revenue from the new operations was fifteen million dollars from the flatbed division and forty million dollars from Bulldog.

Hunt acted on another opportunity that also related to its used equipment. Shortly after announcing the flatbed expansions, Hunt announced the formation of Hunt de

Mexico, Inc., a partnership with Fletes Sotelo of Juarez, Mexico. The joint effort, believed to be the first corporation formed by Mexican and U.S. trucking firms, expanded on informal agreements and trade that Hunt had been conducting with Mexican firms. The new partnership also offered increased placement for Hunt's older tractors.

As the "lousy year" of 1990 drew to an end, some analysts conceded that a truckload firm that could hold its own in the current economic climate had made an accomplishment. Thompson agreed that the truckload companies were just recently catching up to the economic pressures imposed by deregulation on the LTL sector. Though many truckload carriers were in poor shape, Thompson said Hunt, having added four new divisions and operating out of forty offices in the United States, Canada, and Mexico, was a "shining exception to that rule."

A Billion-Dollar Motor Carrier

In December 1990, during one of his enthusiastic lectures to new drivers at the company training school, J. B. Hunt repeated the prediction of corporate growth he said he had been making for the past five years. The company would be the first motor carrier in the world to exceed one billion dollars in annual revenue, and progress toward that goal was currently 5 to 10 percent ahead of schedule, Hunt said.

That month, a *Forbes* magazine article titled "Rough Road" recounted Hunt's glory days in the mid-1980s when its low-cost structure easily won over business from unionized competitors. The magazine detailed Hunt's decline in earnings status, accounting for industry factors such as a soft economy, a driver shortage, and rising costs for fuel and equipment.

But *Forbes* also credited Hunt for its long-term position on driver pay and training and the potential for flatbed operations to capitalize on the market when the construction recession ended. Thompson's remarks ended the article on a note of cautious optimism.

"At some point margins have to stabilize in the industry, and when they do, we're going to be fine . . . We won't go headlong into the storm. We'll make sure our wipers are working. But if we see a chance, we're going to take it."[34]

Within a few weeks, preliminary 1990 financial results were released, reflecting a second year of increased revenue, up to $579.8 million, accompanied by decreased profits, down to $30 million. This time, Thompson took a somewhat philosophical position in explaining corporate progress and potential.

"I wouldn't say we're happy with 1990, but considering the industry, it was pretty good," Thompson said. "It's all relative. The good news is we're ahead of the pack. The bad news is the pack hasn't fared too well."[35]

The corporate goal of increasing annual earnings by 15 percent had not been met in 1990. Yet Thompson said the company had good potential to do so in 1991 based on additional revenues from new operations and freight rates keeping better pace with inflation.

For Paul Bergant, relative stability of the trucking industry and ultimate success for Hunt depends on a sense of business maturity that has only recently begun to develop. Motor carriers have not fully learned the relationship of pricing and equipment capacity, Bergant believes, and leading firms, Hunt among them, have made judgment errors in the past years.

"In the 1980s, we raised prices three or four times, but every time we got a price in, it was temporary," Bergant said. "We'd add hundreds of tractors in a few months, then have to reduce prices to get that fleet moving. So we'd start at ground zero or go below where prices were before they raised."

Hunt maintained stable prices in 1990 because it did not add traffic, Bergant said. But he had doubts about other firms showing similar control.

In the past eighteen months, Hunt raised rates without

adding capacity, but expenses continued to rise. The temptation for the company to add new equipment was tempered by what Bergant believed would be a knee-jerk reaction by competitors to do the same just to keep pace.

"We've got to avoid those cycles," Bergant said. "What happens at the end of the recession will be the tell-tale sign of what the decade of the 1990s has in store for us."

Directions for the 90s

If there was some speculation on the strategy Hunt would pursue in the coming decade, the 1990 annual report laid those questions to rest in no uncertain terms. Titled *Directions for the 90s,* the report opened with a revised mission statement that introduced new terminology and broad corporate horizons.

Hunt would offer "world-class execution" of its customers' logistical needs with "multi-modal, containerizable transportation services to the global marketplace." No longer restricting itself to a position as a national truckload carrier, Hunt had set its sights on world-wide distribution business. It was doing so with the belief that the decade of the 1990s would reward "quality, innovative companies with a return that reflects the risks associated with our business."

In their letter to shareholders, Thompson and J. B. Hunt offered an analytical review of the new strategy. Since 1986, corporate margins had declined more than 50 percent despite the company's advancement in average miles per gallon, driver turnover, equipment utilization, and other key operational facets. The margin erosion, the executives stated, was caused by inflationary costs unaccompanied by proportional increases in freight rates.

Although freight rates increased by only 3 percent in 1990, the Hunt executives expressed an opinion shared by many industry analysts—that 1990 marked an end to a decade of post-deregulation uncertainty. For Hunt, 1990 was a "pivotal year in which the euphoric expansion of capacity and ten years of rising costs gave way to more rational pricing and controlled growth."

Having emerged from the ten-year storm of rate wars and carrier consolidation as the industry leader, Hunt was in no mood to rest on its laurels. With key phrases in its new mission statement pointing the way, the company once again seemed prepared for a major undertaking. In speeches during the year, J. B. Hunt began referring to plans for a dramatic expansion of northwest Arkansas air transport facilities.

When the former truck driver spoke of jumbo jets flying to Springdale from remote locations and unloading containerized cargo onto waiting Hunt vehicles, audiences shook their heads in amazement. And when Hunt suggested that American industry would have to "do more with less" to meet the challenge of international competition, people nodded their heads in agreement.

Thompson focused the corporate direction on more immediate activity. In remarks at the 1990 shareholders' meeting, Thompson said the biggest opportunity for increased business remained in North America and a potential free trade agreement with Mexico. The underlying message was that expansion and diversity would not diminish Hunt's dominance in its core dry van business.

Referring to examples of Japanese business success since World War II, Thompson said a company must enter new markets cautiously, learn how to compete in them, and then seek to dominate the field.

"To be successful in today's environment, an organization must concentrate on increasing revenue by expanding its markets rather than protecting the markets it already has, even at the expense of short-term profits," Thompson said.

The concept of an expanded market was made evident in a new rail-truck partnership announced in June 1991. Hunt extended its intermodal services with a contract with Burlington Northern Railroad. The new service would involve a truck-train loading hub at Chicago and link with exisiting bases in Portland, Oregon, and Seattle. The new relationship with Burlington, in addition to the exisiting Quantum intermodal operations, further established Hunt as a pacesetter in making cooperative agreements between the traditional rival trucking and railroad industries.

Hunt's corporate expansion has been undertaken without an accompanying degree of restructuring or reorganization. Too often, companies shuffle their executives like a deck of cards, assigning new responsibilities and titles, creating new divisions in an attempt to maintain control of a situation. While this exercise does introduce a fresh perspective and offer new experience to senior players, the basic situations and the people who deal with them remain unchanged.

Hunt has embraced change and growth from a more pragmatic position. Its traditional work ethic has been adapted to large-scale corporate challenges. In spite of trucking-industry financial turmoil and a recessive economy, Hunt has set in place a process for long-term development. Having done so in the worst of times, the corporate position in the best of times seems highly promising. A rebounding economy and a more stable trucking industry can only further solidify Hunt's leading role.

4

On the Road with a Hunt Driver

Hunt driver Mike Stier was heading south across the Arkansas River bridge when the sarcastic voice of a driver of a nearby truck came on his CB radio.

"There's old J. B. puttin' down the road, slowing traffic."

Stier grinned and switched the radio off. He held his truck's speed to a steady fifty-five miles per hour while other "large cars" (tractor-trailers) and "four wheelers" (passenger cars) passed him in the left lane.

"I don't listen to the CB much," Stier said. "There's too many distractions, too many rumors I don't need to hear."

In the next two days, Stier would have several occasions to become distracted or frustrated as errors and delays prolonged what should have been an uneventful delivery of freight. And later that night in a phone booth on a desolate street corner in Fort Worth, Stier still maintained a calm disposition as he explained to a distant Hunt dispatcher that the street directions printed on his cargo papers had brought him nowhere near the correct warehouse location.

For despite his job's long hours that dictated when he could eat, sleep, or spend time at home, Stier said he earned nearly forty thousand dollars last year, his second year driving for Hunt. It was a substantial salary, he admitted, for a thirty-three-year-old former factory worker and mechanic with no college education.

But driving out of Little Rock that day, Stier and his passenger had little idea of what awaited them. Up ahead in the blowing fog, the midday traffic was heavy and slow moving. Stier flicked his headlights on and off to signal the passing eighteen wheelers. And he kept his truck a fair distance behind the vehicle ahead as cars darted past in the left lane, then abruptly swung into the right lane before him.

"I don't go faster than fifty-five unless I have to," he continued. "Good fuel mileage makes my fleet manager look good. She takes care of me, so I'll do what I can to make her look good."

Stier talked a lot about his fleet manager, Donna Bridges, during the next two days. He talked to her by phone nearly as often, calling in his times of arrival and departure from customer locations. Other times, as long, idle hours were spent watching warehouse crews slowly fill the trailer, Stier would make periodic calls to Bridges, inquiring about loads that had recently become available or loads that might send him out on profitable long-distance runs to California.

"Donna knows me better than I know myself," he said. "She's a real person, not just a voice. She showed me this company had a heart, that it cared about the drivers. The person behind that desk is J. B. Hunt to me."

Twice recognized as a 1990 Driver of the Month at the North Little Rock terminal, Stier said his driving performance, along with those of thirty-six others assigned to Bridges, determined her overall evaluation. Appreciation for an exceptional fleet manager strongly motivated his efficient driving, he said.

"I'm not a company man," he added. "It's just people I care about."

Stier seemed to enjoy having an audience for the stories and explanations he shared the next two days. Many drivers are talkative by nature, with strong personal opinions they will readily express. Ask a driver how his truck is running, how he might reorganize corporate business, or what is right or wrong with the world today, and these road-seasoned philosophers will begin a lecture that might carry on through the night.

A driver's vocal endurance is fortified by long hours of solitude behind the wheel. When those lengthy periods of silence are replaced by brief encounters in truck stops, terminal break rooms, and loading docks, drivers try to make the most of the moment with jokes and stories, with tales of personal heroism or outrageous events witnessed on the road.

Some of the conversations in the North Little Rock terminal break room earlier in the day could have come from the dime novels of an earlier epoch. One driver who sat across the table from Stier related a tale that had most of those in earshot shaking their heads in astonishment.

The driver, a heavy-set fellow with a large, floppy hat, told how a flatbed driver tried to run him off the road by swinging his vehicle into the Hunt truck from the right lane. The flatbed driver pushed in the Hunt driver's right side mirrors so they reflected back into the cab and were of no use.

"There I was, driving blind on my right side," the Hunt driver told those around him. "I was in the left lane with no way to change over, and up ahead the road narrowed down to a single right-hand lane."

"Just when I thought I was going off the road, another J. B. came up beside me. That driver pulled over close, opened his window, and reached over for my mirrors. He pulled my mirrors straight. Then he took off down the road. I had just enough time to get over before my lane ended in a concrete wall."

Driver stories, like those of soldiers returning from battle, take on new embellishments as they are repeated for different audiences. And similar to other adventurers, the newest drivers are often those with the most outlandish tales to tell.

The older drivers who sat in the break room that morning listened to the story in silence. Others ignored the tale. They watched television and read newspapers or worked on their log books. The break room was large and well lit. It was very clean, and the vending machines offered a variety of packaged food items. But through the haze of cigarette smoke that rose to the ceiling and through the self-promoting tales of the younger drivers' exploits, a more somber atmosphere could be detected.

It was the unspoken recognition of each man's isolation, the collective solitude of strangers within a crowd. Only minimally expressed, it appeared as a spark of interest in their eyes when the television displayed an engaging housewife cheerfully making her pitch for soap or a traditional living-room scene with an attractive woman spraying furniture polish. Each time the drivers quickly glanced up at the television, then let their attention drift back to their newspapers and books.

"Sure, the new driver talks more," Stier said as his truck rolled south on Interstate 30 toward the Texas line. "He's the one with the 'I know everything' attitude. The older, veteran driver won't talk as much. Those are the guys you see wearing the J. B. uniform. They're proud of it."

Stier was wearing his company colors—brown trousers and jacket, tan shirt with a corporate logo patch on the breast pocket. He drove with his seat belt fastened and both hands gently holding the large wheel before him. When the truck bounced over rough spots in the road, the cab's air-cushion seats absorbed most of the shock. There was still enough of a jolt to develop a tightness in the neck and shoulders, a discomfort Stier said usually passed away after the first day of driving.

"Now you're getting the feel of the road," Stier said. "A new driver finds out real quickly all the things they don't tell him in training."

Riding in the cab of a tractor-trailer rig is a unique experience. From that vantage point high above the road, the most spacious passenger cars and vans are considerably below the driver's level. The muffled roar of a diesel engine reverberates through the cab. The forty-eight-foot dry van trailer is a huge box on wheels that will easily tear up corner sidewalks and sign posts when an inattentive driver cuts his turns too sharply.

With responsibility for the largest and most powerful vehicle on the road, a driver has little room or time for his attention to wander. As Stier put it, "You've got to be real careful about these. Run over something and it's likely you won't feel it till you've cost someone a lot of money."

The load that day was twenty-nine thousand pounds of General Mills cereal products. With delivery not due until the next morning, Stier had an easy seven-hour ride ahead of him. His only stop along the way would be a dinner break at the Flying J truck stop northeast of Texarkana.

Stier's day had begun in a normal manner, drinking coffee with other drivers in the terminal break room or visiting with Bridges. Between calls from other drivers, Stier teased her about a load to California she might assign him.

After more than an hour of waiting, Stier's name was called on the intercom. He received his load papers at the dispatch desk and drove his tractor around the terminal yard to locate the assigned trailer. Circling the yard once, Stier found the trailer with the serial numbers he needed. But the loaded trailer was parked on the terminal "shop line" and was scheduled for maintenance work.

Inside the shop area, the head mechanic located the trailer numbers on his computer and called them into a hand radio. After a moment, the radio responded with the voice of another mechanic from somewhere in the large facility. The trailer would not be ready for more than two hours.

Stier returned to the terminal and got in line with other drivers waiting their turns with the dispatch supervisor. One driver was telling jokes about driver trainers and new students. Another said his wife would be very suspicious if he were assigned a female student for driver training. The men were in good spirits. Their paperwork had been cleared and their waiting time was nearly over. They would soon be out of the yard, accumulating miles and earning money.

Stier got his second load assignment and again circled the yard to locate the trailer. To his surprise, it was also on the shop line, a second setback he said he had never experienced before. Nevertheless, he backed his tractor underneath the trailer until the linkage plates locked together. Then he shut off his engine and climbed down from the cab to prepare the trailer for travel.

It was a routine he performed at the start of every trip. He connected the electric and air lines and cranked up the trailer front support legs. He checked air pressure in the tires and brakes and verified that his mud flaps and lights were in working order. Stier then drove to the end of a line of trucks waiting for maintenance crew clearance. He was sixth in line.

Half an hour later, his rig was inside the shop area with a maintenance crew working on the trailer's rear axle. A wheel bearing was found to be low in oil. Another hour was needed to service it.

Back inside the drivers' break room, Stier settled in for another period of waiting. More drivers had arrived and new stories of road hazards and heroism were being exchanged. One fellow was telling of difficulties on a recent trip to New Jersey, a less popular destination for many Midwest-based drivers because of heavy traffic and narrow city streets.

Other drivers were asking about load assignments, hoping to switch trailers for a run near their homes. The drivers were planning several moves in advance, figuring that a load to one destination might set them in place for another choice assignment. Their goal was to get close enough to home so their fleet managers could schedule them an overnight or weekend stay.

Stier said he had been home about every fourth weekend last year. Though only one week past his most recent home stay, he was now speculating how the delivery to Fort Worth might lead to a run heading east, bringing him through

Shreveport and his home across the Red River in neighboring Bossier City.

"There are two different worlds, driving and home," he said. "When you're on the job, you always want to be moving. You're in the trucking mood, making those connections and making the money. Then you get home and get your meals cooked and get hugged on. Then it's hard to get out of bed."

"Sure, I'd like to be a bedbug," he said, referring to short-haul or union trucking jobs where drivers have set schedules and are home several evenings each week. "But there are not many openings, so you've really got to be the best to get those."

"There's no point in me changing to a different long-haul company," Stier went on. "I'd be doing the same work, but I'd lose my seniority."

Other trucking firms were interested in Hunt drivers because of their superior training and driving record, he believed. In the strong competition for recruiting drivers, Stier said he once saw a lady in a bikini working a driver-recruiting effort at a truck stop.

Women are no strangers at truck stops. More women drivers are breaking the male stereotype of the profession, though the traditional roles of waitresses in truck-stop restaurants show little sign of change. As he sipped his coffee in the dining room of the Flying J, Stier spoke about another cadre of women who worked the truck stops.

"You can get to some truck stops and the lot lizards will be all over the CB. They'll ask if you want some company. Then they'll find out what rig you're in and where you're parked. You won't see them inside here."

Prostitution, alcohol, and drugs are the dark side of the truckers' world. For drivers on the road, illicit and dangerous temptations are no less available than in a city. Across the parking lot from the Flying J, the colored neon lights of a liquor store shone brightly. Deep ruts in the grass median between the store and parking lot showed that many drivers had gone directly from one location to the other.

Inside the truck stop, drivers were using the telephones and laundry machines. Many were slouched in front of a television set in the "drivers only" area, the blank expressions on their faces revealing fatigue and boredom. The dining room was an attractive, modern facility that a family would find comfortable. The only distinction was each table had a telephone so drivers could make calls as they waited for their food.

"This is where you can find whatever you're looking for," Stier said as he polished off a generous portion of pork chops and mashed potatoes. "Somebody here will sell you something. Somebody else will tell you what to do so it won't be detected in a drug test."

Stier related these truck-stop options with the same calm acceptance he had shown when driving in the dense fog at Little Rock earlier in the day. He accepted them as something he had to get through, a less attractive part of his world, but one in which he showed little interest or indignation.

On the positive side, truck stops also offer drivers a short time in each other's company to unwind with conversation and laughter. Stier spoke of the jokes and teasing that go on, particularly in smaller truck stops, when a new driver walks in. Something truckers find tremendously funny is watching a novice driver repeatedly circle a yard trying to maneuver his or her rig into a tight parking place.

It was 6:30 P.M., prime dinner time for drivers, and the Flying J parking lot was nearly full. More than one hundred trucks were parked in close ranks, row after row, many with their running lights on and their engines humming loudly. The tight formation of trucks suggested an immense and concentrated power, and the vehicles dwarfed the men who climbed in and out of their cabs.

Stier continued south a few hours until the distant horizon began to glow with lights. Closer to Dallas, the surrounding landscape became more illuminated, and soon the highway had become a wide expressway flanked by businesses and billboards, a network of residential streets and glaring commercial boulevards. The truck rolled through the downtown center, passing skyscrapers and towers outlined in colored lights.

Driving through a city at night is stimulating. City traffic and a profusion of street signs place new demands on a driver's reaction time. With the surrounding darkness reinforcing the driver's solitary mission, the city becomes a milestone of the journey and a time check for his progress. Each city passed in route is a measureable achievement, one step closer to the completed run.

With the lights of Dallas behind him and Fort Worth thirty miles ahead, Stier checked his cargo papers for the freeway exit and street directions he would follow to locate the receiving food warehouse. He had the directions memorized after reading through them a second time. It was nearly ten o'clock, and other trucks were parked for the night in rest stops along the highway.

"Some of these guys will pull into a rest stop for a few hours, pull up right behind another trailer and just lean over the wheel and sleep," he said. "I'll tell you why that's a bad idea. When you wake up, you see the back end of a parked truck right in front of you. You slam on the brakes thinking you're about to run into it. Another thing, I don't want to get used to sleeping in the sitting position."

Stier said fatigue can play tricks on a driver's vision. When drivers do not realize they are tired or push themselves beyond safe limits, they may see things on the road that are not there, like a dog crossing the highway or another truck passing them. To gain additional miles, drivers may try to convince their fleet managers they are ready for another load when they should be resting, Stier added.

"If I forget my limits, Donna's going to put me to bed," he said. "She'll ask how much sleep I got last night. I might say nine hours. Then she'll be real quiet for a while. Next run I get will probably be a short one or have a long layover. I can either sit there all day or go to bed."

When his truck pulled off the highway at Fort Worth, frustration, not fatigue, became the dominant sensation. The instructions on his cargo papers led Stier to a quiet residential neighborhood of private homes and streets far too narrow for his truck. No warehouses or commercial buildings were anywhere nearby.

Stier circled the neighborhood avoiding the narrow streets. He found a nearby hospital parking lot, pulled in and shut the motor off. It was nearly eleven o'clock and a cold wind was blowing. Stier zipped up his jacket and began walking the deserted streets to find the warehouse address.

He walked several blocks, searching the house numbers for 601 7th, the address printed on his papers for the food distributor. He pointed out low branches of trees hanging over the pavement, a sign that no tractor-trailer rigs had driven the street. He finally located a phone booth and called the Hunt terminal for better instructions.

The call to North Little Rock was relayed to a fleet manager at the Dallas terminal who insisted Stier was in the correct location because the fellow's map had a red dot on it there. Stier explained again that he was in a residential neighborhood, but the fleet manager only advised him to park his truck and try to find the warehouse in the morning.

"Great advice," Stier said, as he headed back toward his rig. "By morning, these streets will be full of traffic, and I'll be going nowhere."

Stier walked past a convenience store just as a city police officer drove up. The officer had a city map, and after some searching, he suggested Stier try to locate the warehouse on 7th Street, an industrial area close to downtown. The area he was in now was on 7th Avenue, the officer said.

An hour later, Stier had maneuvered his truck through a maze of city streets and the downtown business center. Having to pass through a railroad yard presented additional complications. Several of the railroad overpasses had two signs stating height clearance. One sign said clearance was 13'4". Right beside it, the other sign said 13'7". The trailer Stier was hauling, like all others in the Hunt fleet, had a clearance of 13'6".

After a quick inspection of the overpass, Stier said he believed he could get through. He put the tractor in first gear and crawled it through the passage, stopping frequently to stand on the side of the cab and visually check his clearance. Both overpass signs were incorrect, and Stier made it through with inches to spare.

When he finally located the Ben E. Keith warehouse, it was 12:30 A.M. and a light frost was settling on the streets. Stier parked the truck directly in front of the closed gates so he would be first in line to unload the next morning. He shut the motor off and slipped out of his shoes, then climbed into the double-wide bunk behind his seat and wrapped himself in blankets. Within minutes, he was fast asleep.

At eight o'clock the next morning when the warehouse crew began to arrive, Stier was standing outside the yard gates talking to another driver who had arrived during the night and parked his rig second in line. Another half hour passed before the crew had the yard gates open and the loading docks ready. Stier backed his rig into place, exactly on time for his scheduled 8:30 delivery. It would be noon before he would drive away.

During the next two hours, while the warehouse crew unloaded and restacked his freight, Stier phoned Bridges at the North Little Rock terminal several times. He had to report his arrival and unloading times, but he was more interested in where his next load would take him. He was hoping for a twelve-hundred-mile run with a Monday morning delivery, California perhaps, something that would let him drive two hundred miles today, and five hundred miles each day of the weekend.

The warehouse break room was a long, narrow chamber with a window that faced a wall stacked with buckets of floor-cleaning solvent. Stier drank coffee or walked out onto the warehouse floor to watch the forklift operators working. The Keith crew worked quickly, but many of the pallets they took from the trailer had to be unwrapped and the individual boxes restacked to meet their inventory system.

Stier joked with the crew as they worked and complimented them on their efforts. Many food warehouse crews require drivers to unload their own trailers and restack the pallets before the load is accepted, he said.

When a food-service truck pulled into the yard, the crew took their morning break. Stier bought a soda and a pastry, his first meal of the day, and sat with the men in the break room. The crew talked briefly about company business, then the jokes about J. B. Hunt began.

The jokes generally began with "Did you hear about the Hunt driver who . . . ," and they ended with punch lines of exaggerated and foolish behavior. One worker told of the driver who steered off the pavement and into a field because he said his left turn signal had gotten stuck. Another told of a Hunt driver who couldn't identify his overturned trailer on the side of the road because he insisted his trailer had its wheels on the bottom.

With no base in reality, the jokes were simple and impersonal, but after each one the warehouse crew looked to the Hunt driver to see his reaction. Stier laughed along with them, then told a few jokes of his own to show he was a good sport. He told the crew that J. B. Hunt joke books were sold in some truck stops. One of the forklift drivers said that before Hunt became the biggest trucking company, all the jokes he heard were about Schneider and Roadway drivers.

Stier's last call to North Little Rock gave him a promising assignment. He was to drive his empty trailer to a paper company south of Dallas and pick up a load heading to Georgia over the weekend. The east-bound run would route him through Shreveport, giving him a night at home. The only complication was in getting his passenger back to the North Little Rock terminal. Bridges said she would work on that during the afternoon.

The slow morning at the Keith warehouse was followed by a short ride to Dallas and an even more tedious afternoon at the paper factory. Arriving at 1:00 P.M., Stier found himself third in line at the loading docks behind two Hunt trucks.

Inside the plant, operations seemed at a standstill with shift workers still not back from lunch.

Though they had never met each other before, the three Hunt drivers began an easy conversation that quickly bridged their personal differences. One was a fifteen-year veteran of northeast short-haul trucking companies who had joined Hunt only three months earlier seeking steadier work. The other driver was an Arkansas native now living in East St. Louis who had been driving for Hunt a few years. The second man boasted that his job had taken him to all forty-eight states and into Canada.

The drivers stood in the plant loading area passing the hours trading stories and watching the trailers being filled. Though they showed little outward concern, each driver carefully watched the forklift operator position the freight inside his trailer. Stier later explained that once a driver signed for his freight, anything damaged in route was his responsibility even if it was a result of poor loading.

"You mess up here, it gets in your pocket real quickly," he said.

Through the afternoon, the Hunt drivers stated their ideas on how the plant workers and equipment could be modified to make trailer-loading operations more efficient. Late in the day, when Stier was the only driver still waiting for his load, the hours seemed to pass with an even greater lethargy. It was "free time," which meant that the long hours waiting in the factory produced no income for him.

It was 6:00 P.M. and growing dark when Stier signed his load papers and sealed the trailer doors. Before getting onto the highway, he stopped at a nearby Dairy Queen and bought a couple of sandwiches. It was the first thing he had eaten since the pastry that morning in Fort Worth. Stier explained that if he had left the factory during the afternoon to get something to eat, he might have lost his spot in line and not gotten loaded until the next morning.

"Maybe now you understand why half of my class was gone three months after we finished driver training school,"

Stier said as he drove east toward Shreveport on Interstate 20. "When I started, I thought I'd quit after the first year. But you get used to the irregular hours. You learn to eat and sleep when the load allows, not when you want to."

It had not been a very profitable day. Stier would have about five hours total driving time when he reached home that night, but he seemed to accept the day's inadequacy within the larger scope of the job. He trusted Bridges to find him the loads that would make up for the day's short runs.

Arriving in Bossier City about 10:30 that night, Stier parked in the pre-arranged spot where Bridges had scheduled a trailer switch with another driver the following day. With his new load, Stier would pass through North Little Rock, drop his passenger off, and then head east to Lexington, Kentucky.

Stier disconnected his rig and drove the detached tractor to his home nearby. He was welcomed by his wife, a friendly, chatty woman who quickly set him up in his recliner chair, offered to cook him dinner, then brought him a cold drink and a bag of his favorite snack food. She gave him the week's mail to review and answered his questions about household projects she had completed.

Candy Stier seemed remarkably competent in her ability to handle domestic affairs. Like other drivers' wives, she had learned how to get things done on her own. But she had been influenced by another occupational condition. Having her husband home after a week of absence, she had much to tell him. She was still telling him when it was time for him to leave the next morning.

"Sometimes when I'm away for a month or so, it takes her three days to unwind," Stier said.

By midday Saturday, Stier was hauling his new load north into Arkansas, expecting to arrive in North Little Rock in the early afternoon. A stretch of Interstate 30 was littered with black scraps of shredded truck tires, "alligators on the road" Stier called them.

The defective tire parts led to a comparison of other rigs on the highway. Among the many trucks were tractors with tall and shiny chrome exhaust pipes, with long-nose engines and flaring bumpers, with double-decker sleeper cabs equipped with skylights and side windows.

"This bus isn't fancy, but it rides well," Stier said about the 1991 International Harvester cab-over tractor he was driving. "It's a trade off of comforts for pay. J. B. told us in training he could put us in a long-nose cab, but our pay would be eighteen cents a mile. So it depends where you want it. In your pocket or here in the cab."

With the Little Rock skyline in the distance, traffic began to grow more congested. From the back window of a passing car, two children waved to Stier and pumped their arms to signal him to blast his air horn.

Stier chuckled and waved back but did not pull on the horn cord that hung from the cab ceiling.

"I'll sometimes blow the horn for kids out on a country road, but in these tight city lanes you don't want to scare Mom or Dad off into the ditch."

Arriving at the North Little Rock terminal, Stier parked his truck and headed for the drivers' break room. A driver might be there willing to switch loads, and Stier was still looking for that trip to California.

5

Operations

Motor-carrier operations can be defined as simply keeping a fleet of trucks loaded with freight and rolling down the highways. But success in the contemporary trucking industry is not achieved by responding to single problems with uncoordinated solutions. Companies that stress individual department efficiency at the expense of inter-department cooperation will find their total effort may not equal the sum of their parts.

In the complex business structure that governs trucking, a more comprehensive operating structure is required. Companies that have the "big picture" will understand that what might seem an unjustified expense in one area can yield a higher return across the entire corporation.

Forbes magazine recognized this strategy in a November 1990 article that said various Hunt programs such as the corporate driver school, the national terminal network, and benefits for drivers have increased annual overhead by some twenty million dollars. The payback for this investment, the magazine added, was seen in less driver turnover, fewer accidents, lower recruiting expenses, and no idled trucks.

In operations, logistics, and marketing, each aspect of

the corporate effort is linked to another through cooperative decision making, a result of what Bruce Jones, a former Hunt chief financial officer, calls a "participatory management team." These coordinated, long-term strategies, labeled "Project Alliance," involve the rewriting of all marketing and operations' computer programs. Paul James, executive vice president of operations, believes the Alliance effort will dramatically change the way Hunt conducts its business.

"Our operating systems basically were a 1982 engine running a 1991 model car," James said. "With Alliance, we're looking at everything from order entry, to dispatch, to financial reports and safety items. And all of it will be tied in to the new on-board computer systems. It's a brand new operating system."

Driver Issues

A group of student drivers were gathered for a special program at the Hunt training school in Lowell. Having driven and studied together for a week, the new drivers were spirited and noisy, and a few moments were needed to get them seated. J. B. Hunt walked to the front of the room and placed his white Stetson hat on a nearby chair. When the former truck driver and auctioneer began to talk, the room quickly grew quiet.

Hunt began a brief review of his life, condensing his remarkable achievements into a few matter-of-fact sentences. Then he shifted attention to the drivers and asked many of them to name their home towns. As a rapport developed, Hunt shifted again and asked a question that triggered a response of surprised and nervous laughter.

"How many in this room are flat broke?" Hunt asked. A few hands were raised among the thirty or more men and women students.

"Well, if you're broke," Hunt continued, working the room like an evangelist, "you're in the best place you could possibly be. Forty years ago I was sitting just where you are now. You can't tell me nothing about being poor. I never made more than four dollars a day till I was twenty-five years old. I know about being broke, and I know about truck driving."

Hunt quickly surveyed the room again. "Now, how many want to get rich?" he asked. Everyone laughed and raised their hands. Hunt laughed with them, and with the smooth delivery of a master salesman, he launched into his speech.

For the next hour, Hunt told his future employees more about truck driving than many of them expected to hear. He talked about irregular hours and time away from home, about hard bunks and fast food, about professional standards and drivers falling victim to bad habits, particularly those that involve money.

"The problem with truck drivers is they get out on the road and start feeling sorry for themselves. They get lonesome," Hunt said. "Then they start throwing their money away on belt buckles, boots, and stuff in the truck stops."

Hunt used many personal anecdotes to bring his message to life. To inspire the students to set goals and save their money, he told them about a new Cadillac he once saw parked outside a truck stop and the promise he made that day to own a car just like it. To encourage better marriage relations, Hunt reminded the students that their personal happiness was far more important than any job.

"Be good to your wife and tell her you love her," Hunt said. "Don't let this truck-driving job take that away from you. If it does, you need to get up and go right out this door."

The corporate emphasis on family is designed for expert drivers as well as new students. Charlie Watts, a Lowell-based driver with more than thirty years' experience, said his wife liked Hunt the best of the companies where he has worked. Her favor had been won, Watts said, by policies such as a dependable pay schedule, a communication system to relay family messages, and the commitment to getting drivers home on Christmas.

Having driven for Hunt the past four years, Watts added

his personal approval to corporate policies to improve driver conditions. The primary benefit, he said, was Hunt's pay scale and the opportunity for drivers with good records to increase base pay by working as a "first driver" or driver-trainer for recent graduates from the corporate school.

Truck driving is hard work, Watts insisted, hard physically because of long hours behind the wheel and the occasional unloading of freight, and hard mentally because of the solitude of family separation and the impatience caused by freight delays. Yet for all the discomforts, Watts accepted the overall balance of work and compensation.

"It's rough being away from home," he said, "but there are no jobs in this part of the country where you can make nearly fifty thousand dollars a year and be home every night."

Successful drivers have a certain temperament, an insatiable desire to get back on the road after a few days home, Watts said. Having given each of his five sons an exposure to the profession, Watts knows firsthand that truck driving does not appeal to everyone.

"I've taken all my boys with me on the road," he said. "I think they found out there's easier ways to make a living."

Paul James said new drivers frequently bring false expectations to the job. Drivers expecting a paid opportunity to see the country are not aware that much of their driving is done at night. Those who think truck driving means freedom from a set time schedule do not understand that deliveries are made at the customer's preferred time, usually first thing in the morning.

"A lot of drivers forget that driving is a professional job," James said.

Project Horizon

To maintain high standards, Hunt has implemented a driver-satisfaction program called Project Horizon. It includes "Operation North Pole," which guarantees that all Hunt drivers get home for Christmas. Coordinating the effort across all Hunt terminals creates a huge logistics problem and has an impact on the corporate operating ratio for December, but the company believes that driver appreciation of the program justifies the effort. Hunt has also arranged for free Thanksgiving dinners at truck stops for its drivers.

Additional family concerns are also addressed in a section of the corporate newsletter titled "Family Ties." Here, drivers' wives share common experiences of maintaining households and raising children when husbands are not around. And once a year, each Hunt terminal sponsors a "Family Appreciation Day" when wives and children are invited to the facilities for a picnic and entertainment.

Project Horizon deals with the professional environment as well. A Driver Retention Team has been established to address driver concerns and reduce turnover. The team, a mix of drivers and corporate personnel, has had several recommendations implemented, including a home program for co-drivers to reduce new career impact, driver opinion cards for commentary about pick-up points, driver roundtable meetings, and driver birthday and anniversary screens on fleet-manager computers. The Hunt driver policy includes awards for safety and accident-free miles.

The company uniform distinguishes Hunt drivers from their counterparts at other trucking firms. The corporate uniform, brown trousers and khaki shirt, is worn by drivers who must be clean shaven at all times, even when they are several weeks out on the road. No beards, short pants, tee shirts, or tennis shoes are allowed.

How the uniform policy was implemented is one of J. B. Hunt's most entertaining stories and one he includes in speeches to driver-school students. The story is set in the early 1980s, when the Hunt transport division had been operating for more than a decade without making a profit.

"I was out in the dispatch yard one day," Hunt tells the students, "when a driver came along wearing blue jeans cut off at the knees and unraveled to create a ball of fur. He's got a long beard, all stiff and shiny with beeswax, and he's wearing tennis shoes and a tee shirt.

"This guy got in one of our brand new trucks and drove off. I went up to the yard manager and said what's going on here will never work. I told him to shut the gates and not let another man leave until we had fixed this problem."

Hunt said the day the corporate policy barring long hair and beards was implemented, so many people shaved and got their hair cut, it stopped up the entire Lowell sewage system. He tells drivers that from that day onward, the transport division has consistently made a profit.

Bob Ralston, executive vice president of maintenance, tells the story with an added flair, recalling a comment from Hunt at the time that a man so poorly dressed ought to be pushing a wheelbarrow with a flat tire, not entrusted with an eighty-thousand-dollar piece of equipment.

"The story of the poorly dressed driver has been highly embellished," Kirk Thompson insists. "The dress code was voluntary for several months, but those who wanted to drive new equipment had to have company colors on. I don't remember us ever shutting the gates on anyone or anyone who wore a beard."

In response to driver suggestions, a new flexibility has been introduced into the uniform policy, Thompson said. Drivers are still required to be clean shaven, but they are allowed to wear jeans or other clothes on some occasions. The company uniform is still the recommended dress when drivers are on shipper premises, Thompson said.

A New Career

Student drivers in the Hunt training program come from diverse backgrounds. Though generally in their mid-thirties and married, the thirty new students who arrive at Lowell each week represent all levels of education and professional skills. Approximately 15 percent are women. According to school director Jim Ginn, commitment to the program is their most common factor.

"They come here looking for a new career," Ginn said. "The majority have researched it and made an intelligent decision. They're dedicated to it before they start."

Recruited at Hunt terminals across the country, new students meet entry requirements in employment background and driving history. They pass physical exams and interview criteria. And they sign a contract committing themselves to nearly three months of training in exchange for a guaranteed position as a Hunt driver when they succesfully complete the program. The training is provided at no cost to students other than a week's food and lodging in Lowell and the price of their first Hunt uniform.

"I lay down the rules on Monday morning and they sign off on the contract," Ginn said. "We run it as a business and teach the seriousness of the industry."

All students complete a four-week classroom program on federal regulations, logging procedures, hazardous-materials handling, and customer relations. The first week of training is conducted at Lowell, where corporate philosophy and Hunt driver standards form a large portion of the curriculum.

Ginn conducts the final class of first-week training as a graduation program. He takes the occasion to remind drivers of the many choices they will face in the future. He talks about balancing home time and professional demands, about recruitment efforts by other carriers, about career goals and management of personal finances.

At times, the lecture leaves trucking topics completely and addresses family relationships and morality. At the end of the talk, each student is presented with a Hunt cap and pin. Each driver also receives a Bible with the yellow Hunt logo on the cover and a national listing of Transport for Christ chapel locations.

Classroom training and driving practice continue for another three weeks at driver home terminals. Defensive driving and accident prevention are stressed, as well as time management and awareness of fatigue. The students learn how a driver can be "out of hours" when he has met the federal limit on driving ten hours a day. And they learn to keep fleet managers informed of their status.

The first month training ends with a road test and the federal Commercial Drivers License test. Students then become "second drivers" and spend a seven-week period on the road with a driver trainer.

"Driver trainers know the company and teach the pride factor," Ginn said. "You've got to know who you are and who you work for to have that pride. The enthusiasm is contagious."

One final road test follows before the students become fully certified. The company believes its lengthy and detailed training program has contributed to lower accident rates and reduced driver turnover. Program expenses, approximately one thousand dollars per student help Hunt avoid driver shortages.

Training drivers to understand emotional influences and distractions helps prepare them for their demanding occupation. Hunt tells students that a casual approach to driving does not work. Driving a long run requires a detailed plan of daily mile quotas and scheduled rest stops.

"You've got to act like a professional," Hunt said. "You've got to train yourself to do this job or it will eat you up and burn you out."

Attracting Experienced Drivers

A driver pay-scale increase in November 1990 made Hunt the highest paying truckload carrier in the industry. The new pay scale offered thirty-three cents per mile for drivers with eight years' experience. The strategy behind the raise was to attract experienced drivers and overcome continuing industry-wide shortages.

Experienced drivers tend to be more stable employees.

They have a lower turnover rate than those who have just entered the industry and must work for less pay. With about 80 percent of Hunt drivers still relatively new, the increased pay scale is expected to form a more secure driver base over the next few years.

"We've had significant periods of driver shortages in 1985, 1987, and in the summer of 1990," James said. "Our equipment utilization was affected significantly and 2 to 3 percent of the fleet was open. Our response each time was to pay the drivers more money. We know it's a tough job out there and we have to pay to get that job done."

Hunt has introduced other policy changes to help recruit experienced drivers, including raising the vehicle speed limit to sixty-five miles per hour where allowed on interstate highways and eliminating a weekly mile guarantee that had become confusing. The new policies have brought Hunt a surplus of drivers at times.

"What we are trying to do is provide jobs to people that want to improve themselves," J. B. Hunt told a student-driver class. "Our drivers expect us to be the leading truckline in the nation. I expect our drivers to be the best on the road. How are you going to get something good without paying for it? Cheap truck drivers is not the way you make money."

Tractors and Trailers

The Hunt decision to develop a corporate fleet and employ company drivers was made shortly after deregulation increased trucking-industry awareness of operational cost efficiency. Kirk Thompson recalled J. B. Hunt coming into his office about that time and commenting on the need to reduce fuel expenses.

"He didn't have the answers, but he did have the challenge and the sense of an opportunity out there," Thompson said. "So we attacked that opportunity to get better fuel mileage."

The move to company trucks was a strategic decision. The industry trend in 1980 was toward greater use of owner-operators, and about 50 percent of Hunt drivers were independent truckers. Yet when Thompson and Wayne Garrison began a profitability analysis, they realized that company-owned trucks offered higher margins. Company trucks, because of standardization and new engine technology, were simply more fuel efficient. They also helped establish the corporate image that distinguished Hunt from its competitors at that time.

Hunt bought its trucks from International Harvester, a firm that experienced financial troubles and changed its name in the early 1980s to Navistar. The purchase of 277 Navistar trucks and 1,000 Lufkin trailers in 1983 established a continuing relationship between Hunt and two manufacturers.

"Right at the time they were desparate, we decided to buy all Navistar tractors and no one else's," J. B. Hunt said. "Those hard times glued us together. We helped them and they helped us."

Currently, Hunt's two-to-one ratio of trailers to tractors allows a high degree of equipment flexibility. The large number of trailers allows "drop and hook" operations, where trailers are left at a shipper's yard for loading or unloading at a more convenient date. Loaded trailers can also be stored at Hunt terminals or shuttle yards for delivery at a later date.

Hunt has begun replacing its standard forty-eight-foot trailers with fifty-three-foot models. The newer trailers are especially well suited for lightweight or bulky freight, common shipments in the retail industry. Offering an additional 416 cubic feet, the longer trailers can carry more pallets, and more freight can be loaded per trailer without exceeding axle weight limits. The extra space also translates into reduced dock congestion because nine fifty-three-foot trailers do the same work as ten forty-eight-footers.

Similar operational efficiency is evident in Hunt tractors. The corporate model is a cab-over unit with a recessed front axel. This style allows a better turning radius and driver visibility than "long-nose" tractors, Ralston said. Tractor cabs have uniform interiors, a no-frills decor of vinyl paneling that allows quick cleaning, he added.

Hunt tractors get nearly 7 miles per gallon, a notable increase over the 1978 average of 3.8 miles per gallon. Fuel accounts for approximately 15 percent of total operational costs, so even small gains in fuel efficiency can produce substantial savings. For example, an average one-tenth-of-a-mile-per-gallon increase across the fleet can yield a one-hundred-thousand-dollar-per-month savings.

Ralston credited gains in fuel efficiency to standardized equipment and maintenance, as well as engine improvements in the company's newer trucks. As a result, Hunt vehicles do not emit thick clouds of diesel soot, he said.

"Smoke is unburned fuel, something you won't see in our trucks," Ralston said. "When you see a truck smoking, it usually means the driver hasn't changed his air filters or he's jacked up his fuel pumps for faster speed."

Low regard for maintenance and equipment can also result in the dangerous residue of shredded tires on a highway. These black strips of rubber endanger motorists. They also represent a significant expense to the trucking firm. For Hunt, tires are the third most costly item on the corporate balance sheet after labor and fuel. Truck tires, mounted on 24.5- or 22.5-inch wheels, stand about 3.5 feet high, higher than eye level in most passenger vehicles.

Tires that have been recapped three or four times are more prone to breakdown, so Hunt has a two-recap limit on all its tires. Front steering tires generally achieve 1,000,000-mile life, while rear axel tires can function for up to 240,000 miles. Steering tires, once recapped, are never remounted in the steering position on a truck.

Total vehicle maintenance is tracked by computer, and fleet managers are responsible for routing equipment into the terminals for regularly scheduled work. Hunt maintains seven full-service shops among its many terminals, so scheduled maintenance is rarely restricted by a truck's location.

"We're running one to two million miles a day across the fleet," Ralston said. "But you'll rarely see one of our trucks written up for a safety violation."

With a 25 percent average annual equipment turnover, Hunt puts more than a thousand new trucks on the road each year. In addition to the operational efficiency of new models, the large-scale renewal effort reduces driver dissatisfaction with aging equipment.

The cost of a new tractor will vary with its engine components and other factors, but prices can range from sixty to ninety thousand dollars. Ralston declined to state a price for Hunt's new trucks, but he conceeded that the company receives discounts because of its volume purchases.

Ralston was not hesitant, however, about dispelling a trucking-industry rumor that Hunt had a buy-back agreement that assured a resale market for its used equipment. "We have no buy-back agreements with anyone," he insisted. Instead, the company maintains a five-year depreciation schedule where truck value is reduced by 20 percent each year.

Most vehicles achieve 3 years of service, averaging 130,000 miles per year, before they are traded in or reassigned to short-haul operations. Short-haul divisions such as Quantum and Bulldog help Hunt maintain a young transport fleet with relatively low maintenance costs. Tractors that have completely fulfilled their domestic service potential are marketed to foreign countries or broken down for recycling.

Terminals

Unlike the freight terminals used by LTL carriers, Hunt's nationwide terminal network does not break down trailer loads of freight for resorting and delivery. Activity at Hunt terminals focuses instead on two of the primary components of truckload operations: vehicle maintenance and driver relations.

Hunt's terminal network is a relatively new undertaking.

Until 1985, Lowell was the single base of operations. Since then, fifteen additional terminals have been established across the country. Seven are large "hub terminals" with full maintenance facilities. Smaller regional terminals mainly provide driver services. Hunt also maintains sixteen "shuttle yards" where trailers are parked for shipper convenience. The company maintains a flexible approach to terminal operations. It has closed some locations to enhance alignment with market conditions and driver availability.

The Houston terminal is the company's largest, home base for more than 450 trucks and over 600 drivers. Some 50 tractor-trailers enter and depart the yard every day. As each vehicle comes in, fleet supervisors record mileage and other information on terminal computers, which automatically alert maintenance staff to the specific work required. Each truck is assigned a computer code that flags the vehicle for scheduled maintenance. With facilities for twenty-four thousand-mile oil changes or two hundred thousand-mile rear end services, hub terminals at Houston, Lowell, and other areas provide all vehicle service needs.

This self-sufficiency creates a highly efficient, one-stop environment for the trucks and their drivers. In *Rare Breed,* a 1985 book on American entrepreneurs, J. B. Hunt explained how terminal operations are linked to overall corporate performance.

"While our trucker is having his shower at our terminal, the truck is having its bath. We want them both to be happy and clean because they are the Hunt team. That's another reason for standardized equipment. The drivers are accustomed to the same working environment. This improves their confidence and comfort, and it improves safety and efficiency."

Conducting a brisk tour of the Lowell facility, Maintenance Manager Larry Knapp pointed out the twelve bays of the tractor maintenance shop where complete engine replacement can be performed in about eight hours. Several vehicles were being worked on that day, their large cab frames tilted forward to expose the three-hundred-horsepower, six-cylinder engines. Maintenance crews worked under and inside the huge engines, wielding oversized wrenches and leverage bars that made the crew members seem small in comparison.

Knapp proceeded to a busy area where three tractors were parked over parallel service pits. Brown-suited maintenance teams swarmed around them engaged in a variety of tasks. The activity had a military precision to it, with each worker absorbed in his or her assigned role and a shop foreman overseeing their diverse efforts.

"Our pit-stop area is based on a race-car pit-stop system," Knapp explained. "We can do all maintenance and repairs, front-end and tire work, in less than an hour."

Knapp walked through the open, airy terminal, identifying the engine-rebuilding room, the tractor body shop, the trailer-rebuild facility, and the vehicle paint and washing areas. He described motor-oil analysis tests Hunt uses to assess the breakdown levels for the lubricant. And he explained how engine air filters are cleaned and flushed to extend their service.

Knapp finally came to the fuel-injector room, a closed area whose white walls and spotless floor gave it the atmosphere of a testing laboratory. Inside, Knapp picked up a metal object the size of a desk stapler and demonstrated how the plunger and barrel of a diesel injector work. The unit, machine tooled to a .0002-inch tolerance, allows the plunger to slide smoothly through the barrel opening without the slightest variance or wobble. The precision fit is necessary, Knapp explained, to achieve the eighteen-to-one fuel compression ratio that ignites diesel fuel. Gasoline in regular automobiles ignites at an eight-to-one compression ratio, he added.

Outside in the terminal yard, rows of trucks were parked on either side of the maintenance building. Some were waiting to pass through the facility and receive their scheduled work. Others had completed their inspections and were ready for drivers and freight assignments.

In the yard and maintenance areas, vehicles receive priority treatment. Inside the terminal, however, the emphasis shifts to meeting driver needs and providing all amenities possible. Showers and laundry machines are available, and a free shoe-polish machine offers a subtle reminder of the corporate emphasis on a driver's professional appearance.

In the hallway outside the driver lounge, a long wall is covered with photographs of all Lowell-based drivers. The photos are arranged in chronological order based on date of hire. The number one and two positions at Lowell, and in the entire corporation, are occupied by Lonnie and Tom Whitman, twin brothers who have been driving for Hunt since 1977. The Whitman photos and many others have gold stickers indicating the drivers' years or miles of accident-free driving.

Terminals serve as a driver's home base and a center for recruiting new drivers in the area. A driver's actual home may be a few hours away from the base terminal, but the distance usually seems short after several weeks on the road and thousands of miles driven.

Communications

Over the years, the title *dispatcher* has been changed to *driver supervisor* to the current title of *fleet manager.* The tools of the trade have been upgraded from chalk boards and note pads to computer screens and light-weight telephone headsets. In the near future, satellite systems and on-board computers will instantly relay truck location and performance data.

Despite the sophisticated technology, the job of fleet managers has not significantly changed since the first Hunt truck drove away from the Lowell terminal to receive its freight.

Communication between drivers and fleet managers is a basic part of the Hunt operating system. When a driver calls in to report arrival at a customer site or unloaded status, the phone conversation gives the fleet manager the chance to make new load assignments. At the same time, fleet managers must understand the personal factors that might be influencing the driver. They must listen carefully for suggestions of frustration or fatigue during the conversation.

Some drivers are blunt and expressive about their feelings. Others are less open. The fleet manager has to know the drivers and be able to interpret their comments. With many calls coming in at once, they must be able to efficiently manage their telephone time. Fleet managers also serve as the communication link between a driver and the driver's family, and they frequently pass on messages from home.

"The driver relies on us," Kevin Campbell, a fleet manager at Lowell, said. "We get him his loads and we get him back here on his due-home date. We're his only link to the company, so I've got to give him my full attention and make sure he knows his work is appreciated."

At each Hunt terminal, fleet managers monitor driver performance and link available personnel with new freight assignments. Each manager is in charge of up to forty-five drivers, all working on different schedules as they deliver freight to diverse shipper locations.

In coordination with marketing-department personnel, fleet managers try to get a driver assigned a new load before the current load is delivered. Ideally, the driver will make only one call to report arrival and get a new assignment. For this to happen, fleet managers must keep up with large amounts of constantly changing information.

Marketing-department personnel have information about available trucks and freight that must be delivered. But it is the fleet manager who must match those assignments with an available driver who has not reached the federal hour limit.

"We don't want a driver to push past the limits of the law or his own limits," Campbell said. "If a driver is out of hours, he sits. Even if he has hours left but he's too tired, I'll shut him down."

Large marker boards in the fleet manager's work area

show fleet averages in blue or red numbers, indicating performance above or below goals. Managers are evaluated on driver performance, including turnover, Campbell said, so they must understand how to motivate drivers without pushing them too hard.

"The only thing you can do is support them," Campbell said. "If they're doing a good or bad job, I'll tell them. I'll never tell a driver how to operate a truck, but I can show him what others have done. I've got to keep him trained on the way the company wants this equipment handled. You can pick up a lot of bad habits on the road."

Fleet managers conduct regular performance reviews with drivers, keeping them informed of statistical information on their fuel mileage, engine idle time, and speed above posted limits. Much of this information is maintained by Tripmaster computers, monitoring devices installed in Hunt tractors that provide summary information of vehicle usage. Fleet managers also review less analytical performance factors such as on-time service and maintenance of driver logs and freight invoices.

Getting drivers home on their requested due-home dates is crucial to maintaining positive attitudes, Campbell said. That scheduling responsibility sometimes forces a fleet manager to scan marketing-department computer reports to arrange a suitable delivery for the driver.

"I get frustrated if marketing can't support that, but we've got to remember that the system works overall and sometimes an individual has to make sacrifices," Campbell said. "If you let that happen a few times, you'll lose the driver. And we've got too much time and money invested . . . to let that happen."

Fleet managers also compete with one another to arrange the best assignments for their drivers. They know drivers dislike layovers and short runs, so choice deliveries, such as long-haul West Coast assignments, are eagerly sought after, Campbell said.

"If I don't catch that load, another fleet manager will," he added.

In the mid 1980s, Hunt experimented with telephones in truck cabs to improve driver communication. The system was unsuccessful because phone lines couldn't be opened for all drivers at the same time. Telephone calls across the corporation increased to nearly forty-five thousand calls per day by 1990. To meet this challenge, Hunt installed a Software Defined Network, a special call-routing system utilizing IBM voice response units for driver check calls. Minimizing driver hold and conversation time, the system saved the company approximately $120,000 per month.

Yet the need remained for an efficient communication system that could relay driver information, particularly exact location, to base terminals and corporate headquarters. So in 1991, Hunt entered an agreement with IBM to develop a satellite and computer network that would put a transmitter in every vehicle.

The twenty-million-dollar project, to be implemented in 1992, would provide two-way tracking between drivers and fleet managers, as well as in-truck processing of critical information such as engine operation, temperature, and oil usage. This mechanical data, relayed to Hunt terminals, will help those facilities better prepare for the maintenance the in-coming truck will need. Additional features being considered for the system include driver information on fuel stops, local street maps and directions to customer sites, automatic logging, and bar-coded freight scanners that drivers can use to count freight loaded onto the trailer.

The satellite project will play an increasingly important role as Hunt targets the shorter length-of-haul market. In 1990, more than half of the company's freight deliveries required less than 750-mile runs. And dramatic growth opportunities have been recognized in the 100- to 500-mile length-of-haul market. As transaction intensity increases with these shorter runs, the satellite system will alleviate communication bottlenecks and make it easier for Hunt to know exactly where its trucks are at any moment.

The payoff of this advanced communication link is excellent customer service, an area Hunt has spared no expense to develop. Tom Sanderson, a marketing services vice president, believes the on-board computer (OBC) and satellite system can elimate the traditionally weakest link in the total delivery process.

"The customer demands that we deliver the product on time, but when we only hear from a driver once or twice a day, we don't know a shipment is going to be late until we get the call," Sanderson said. "With OBC, we will know how far a guy can go before he has to break to comply with federal regulations. We'll know in advance if he's not going to be able to deliver on time. So we may get another team out there and swap loads with him. We can get that load in on time without the customer ever knowing what we went through."

Like the entire Hunt executive team, Sanderson has great faith in technology. He was instrumental in developing Hunt's electronic data interchange (EDI) system, a process that allows mainframe computer interaction between Hunt and its largest customers. The EDI system allows for electronic billing and fund transfers, as well as on-line shipment status reports.

The importance of EDI was highlighted in a 1990 article in *Transportation Journal* where the computer link was called a "requirement for doing business" because of its ability to reduce transaction costs and time of execution. The article stated that EDI allows shippers to better monitor carrier service and operating performance, and it noted that the trucking firms using EDI were the industry's largest carriers with the most advanced operating systems.[1]

For the Hunt customer without the size or computer resources to use EDI, a scaled-down version known as PACE (Preferred Automated Customer Exchange) has been developed. PACE is a software package for personal computers that provides much of the same information as EDI. It reduces telephone communication and paperwork with an on-line delivery of electronic billing and shipment status information. PACE has been installed at more than two hundred customer locations, Sanderson said.

Regardless of the size of the customer computer, integrated information systems will provide an increasingly important level of service. Hunt plans on using on-board computers, EDI, logistical support, and other innovative tools. According to Thompson, the movement of information may soon become as critical to shippers and carriers as the movement of freight.

Quality and Customer Relations

Outstanding customer relations and an internal commitment to quality are complementary facets of corporate operations. Virtually every company of size has a structured program where quality improvement teams coordinate input from all levels of the corporate hierarchy to achieve a more efficient performance.

In some cases, these efforts aim to improve internal conditions such as employee job satisfaction or time required for specific tasks. Other quality programs strive for greater customer satisfaction. But quality programs rarely identify immediate cost savings as a primary goal, so an objective analysis of their success may be difficult to obtain.

The Hunt program for quality improvement has been in place since the early 1980s, but in recent years a more comprehensive and formal approach has been taken. Based on results from 1990 alone, the new strategies are working better than ever. During the year, Hunt received awards of excellence and "Carrier of the Year" awards from nine shippers, including Reynolds Metals, Ford Motors, Apple Computers, and Brown and Williamson.

Representative of the service commitment that earned these awards, Hunt handled more than nine thousand truckload shipments for Reynolds Metals, coordinating service between fifty-five Reynolds sites and sixty vendor locations. Ford Motor Company, presenting Hunt with its "Transportation Award of Excellence," said the Arkansas carrier had been selected from more than two hundred transportation companies in a variety of service areas.

The starting point for the corporate quality initiative, Thompson believes, was the introduction in 1983 of management training programs in half-day Saturday sessions. Wayne Garrison was responsible for the initial Hunt management classes, a form of professional training relatively unknown to the trucking industry at that time, Thompson said.

"I give Wayne a lot of credit for this," Thompson said. "He realized early on that we would not get to be a large company by remaining a one-man show. We had to have well-trained, quality people. That thinking was not typical in the trucking industry. Trucking company managers were not being well prepared for the future."

Since 1984, Hunt has offered in-house management training to newly recruited college graduates. Interviewing potential employees from schools with good transportation programs, Thompson said he looks at more than a candidate's strong academic achievement.

"I'm looking for someone with a good work background, someone with ethics, someone who will look you in the eye and talk to you," he said. "I have a standard question about what you liked best in school. Many people tell me about their classes. I gravitate toward those that talk about people and the college atmosphere."

The need for capable people to implement fresh ideas was reiterated by Steve Palmer, executive vice president for human relations. Though the Hunt management approach appeared to be working, the executive team realized early on that "whatever works today probably won't work tomorrow," Palmer said.

The increasing size of the company presented the most immediate problems. Previously, new drivers were able to meet and talk with J. B. Hunt. Now video tapes are used to give new drivers an impression of the chairman. Executive travel and personal contact were encouraged, but the most effective results have been achieved by bringing new people to Lowell for orientation, then returning them to their home areas to instill corporate values in others, Palmer said.

In 1991, the Hunt "Quality in Motion" program was established. Borrowing its title from a successful marketing department campaign, Quality in Motion became a corporate-wide effort for excellence and error-free service. The program's stated goal was to prepare the company to apply for the Malcolm Baldrige National Quality Award.

Similar to the driver retention teams that were formed a year earlier, four quality improvement teams were established in areas of on-time service, worker's compensation, safety, and proof of delivery. An employee telephone hotline was installed to improve internal communication, and a management mentor project was begun, pairing experienced management personnel with new employees to help them overcome initial problems.

Hunt's comprehensive quality programs aim to develop qualities similar to those found in the company's best customers. According to Bergant, Hunt's ideal customers are shippers who adopt a long-term corporate philosophy of excellence. This entails automating as much of the administative process as possible, but more significantly, it reflects a willingness to change and to address problem areas.

"The ideal customer will require a level of service that will keep us on our toes," Bergant said. "At the same time, they will talk to us about any problems that come up. They won't hide from a problem, even when it is their own."

Through its quality programs, Hunt has imposed these ideal aspects on itself. While the programs are still too new to have achieved quantitative results, recent reports of office and division-level efficiencies indicate a promising future.

Again, a comparison to external relations shows how Hunt seeks every opportunity to develop quality operations. The company has established partnerships with Truckstops of America, Unical Systems, and some independent truck stops to provide Hunt drivers with fuel discounts and special amenities. By negotiating for nation-wide discounts, Hunt has been able to secure for its drivers some of the savings and comforts it provides at its own terminals.

6

Logistics

Basic business principles of supply and demand and operating ratio have had slow application in the trucking industry. Only in recent years have advanced economic theories and generic management practices been recognized for their advantages in effecting a smooth flow of customer services.

For shippers, the process of distributing goods requires more than just arranging for transportation services. Shippers must coordinate inventory, warehouse locations, and quality of delivered merchandise. To do this effectively, they require responsive, on-time transportation from carriers.

"Deregulation was important to truckers and shippers," John Ozment, a University of Arkansas transportation professor, said, "but the evolution into logistics would have happened anyway. Understanding that direction is critical to trucking industry management."

Ozment believes that high-quality service is merely a buzz word for many trucking firms who still believe they can maintain strong business relations without upgrading their techniques for meeting customer needs.

"Quality carriers are picking up on the need for more

aggressive customer service, and surviving companies will stress a role in logistics." he said. "Companies that don't understand the importance of doing that will fall by the wayside.

Ozment agreed that premium service necessitates a premium price, but trucking firms can show their customers what the higher rate will buy. They can relate higher freight costs to lower costs in inventory, particularly for just-in-time manufacturing. Damage control and increased customer satisfaction are additional opportunities for reduced costs.

In response to industry needs, most university transportation programs train potential trucking managers in logistics skills. But the academic exercises of the classroom may seem like child's play when a college graduate encounters the demanding world of truckload operations.

"This is not a forty- to forty-five-hour-per-week job," Jeff Franco, Hunt's senior vice president for logistics, said. "Our logistics managers work all week, then put in a twelve-hour shift one Saturday each month."

Hunt logistics managers serve a middle role between operations and marketing. When the marketing department sends order information to logistics, the manager will match single or team drivers to the load then communicate the order to a fleet manager who tells the assigned drivers when and where to pick up the load.

A Hunt logistics manager might start the day at a 6:00 A.M. meeting with customer service representatives. The early meeting lets managers learn the latest scheduled freight deliveries without interfering with peak hours of supervisory responsibility. Once aware of the number of trucks and number of loads in an area, a logistics manager will begin coordinating the two to meet customer expectations.

"This is not really a black and white job. It takes a lot of professional judgement," Franco said. "To be a survivor, you've got to be a risk taker because the solutions to your problems are not always in the most obvious ways."

Occasions will arise when customer service needs exceed the capacity of drivers or equipment immediately available in the area. Then the logistics manager must arrange for more trucks or double-team drivers to expedite the deliveries. A coast-to-coast priority shipment, for example, might require "slip seating," the Hunt process of keeping a load moving by replacing drivers who have completed their allowed time with drivers who can take the truck further on toward its destination.

As the logistics manager coordinates these arrangements, he must be prepared for messages from fleet managers about delays that drivers may have encountered. The logistics manager must notify the customer or the service representative about any schedule changes.

"Everything can change from one minute to the next," Franco said. "You can't just hit your computer keyboard and get your best options. The system gives you the data, but it doesn't program the data. You have to optimize it."

With information on orders, equipment, delivery times, and driver due-home dates, logistics managers must learn how to "juggle a lot of balls," Franco said. They also need a good knowledge of geography and the driving times within their assigned regions. But most importantly, he added, they must be sensitive to personal issues and be able to maintain a positive team relationship among many employees who have never met each other.

Adding to the complexity of their roles, logistics managers must also strive for the lowest possible level of backhauls or "dead-head" miles, which is the distance an empty truck must travel between loads. Because carriers get paid only for the miles a loaded truck travels, empty miles can very quickly influence profitability.

Hunt's size is a strong advantage in this area. With its large number of trucks and widely developed customer base, new freight assignments at nearby locations can be located for virtually every empty truck and available driver. The responsibility for this coordination belongs to logistics managers and fleet managers who must function on a national scale as efficiently as they do regionally.

A decreasing length of haul is another operational factor influencing the logistics manager's job. With more than half of Hunt's 1990 loads traveling less than 750 miles, more complex transactions and more loads are required to conduct the same amount of business as when average length of haul was longer. As a result, logistics managers have a larger number of variables to coordinate on a day-to-day basis.

Logistics managers now have direct contact with all terminals. Part of their responsibility is to know where every load is, when it is to be picked up, and when it is to arrive at the receiver's site. This base of knowledge has been tremendously influenced by computer technology. The Hunt plan for satellite transmission of in-cab computer data will advance the process even more.

Bruce Jones believes the satellite system will allow the company a fundamental leap in quality of service. Presently, management has control of the process only when drivers call in from a customer site or en route. Jones estimates this contact period to be approximately 15 percent of the total process. The remainder of the time, the company has no way of knowing a driver's location, his mental attitude, the weather or traffic he is experiencing. And highway accidents may delay a driver's phone call by several hours.

These variables place the company in a reactive positive, Jones believes. Through technology, however, he anticipates a comprehensive review process, a mechanism that tracks real-world variables 100 percent of the time and gives the company a strategic advantage in customer service and equipment utilization.

"Growth forced us to accept complexity," Jones said. "We can never totally remove the variables, but we can develop sophisticated tools to use them to our advantage."

7

Marketing

Until 1990, Hunt's marketing strategy primarily had targeted the single objective of building transport operations to maximum size and efficiency. Through the rate wars of the 1980s, key decisions to standardize fleet operations and enhance driver services allowed the company to grow and prosper at a level that far outdistanced its truckload competitors.

With 1990 revenue of nearly $580 million, Hunt still recognized tremendous growth potential in the estimated $18 billion dry van truckload market. But the year's annual report weighed that potential in relation to a more immediately achievable goal.

"It remains unclear how much of the total market share we want. In 1990, we began to realize that not all truckload freight is good freight for J. B. Hunt. In the future, we want only the freight that will give us stronger profits than we've experienced in the last two years."[1]

The decision to limit marketing efforts to the most profitable sector of the truckload industry was matched by a commitment to diversify corporate activity. New transportation options, both nationally and internationally, have been established. This new base of operations offers a similar potential to what Hunt faced ten years earlier—a competitive environment whose players generally lacked a coordinated strategic approach.

Predictably, Hunt's entrance to these new markets has been guided by the same principles that yielded its previous success. Hunt's current competitive advantage in size, financial stability, and quality service has been achieved by an executive group that functions as a team. This cooperative ability can be traced back to J. B. Hunt's sense of shared responsibilities.

"God didn't give everybody the talent for everything," J. B. Hunt said. "You have to go out and find people different than you are to run these companies. It takes a different kind of guy to think about something and see way down the road versus a guy that's really going to have to go in there and do the detail work."[2]

Teamwork is extolled by every corporation. But many firms misunderstand that sincere cooperative attitudes must be manifest on the executive level if they are to be adopted throughout the corporate structure. Executive lip service may convince those who recite the words but few others. Questioned on the factors of Hunt's success, Thompson suggested such was not the case at Lowell.

"We generally say it's a matter of executing. It doesn't depend on superstars. It depends on everybody being role players and doing the best of what they are supposed to be doing and helping each other and the team atmosphere. It's living out your culture or personality in everyday activities that fosters that open team spirit."[3]

For Jones, teamwork is a matter of trading specific technical skills for broad-based management skills, creating what he calls "technical generalists," people with superior technical knowledge who can do a variety of things. The result, he said, is a staff many times smaller and considerably more versatile than might be found among Hunt's competitors.

"In the past, there was not a lot of joint discussion and input into issues," Jones said. "Now we're of such size and complexity that virtually anything that happens will have an impact on another department. With a small corporate staff, one person may not have the answers, but he can help facilitate how we all think about things."

Teamwork builds pride in achievement. At Hunt, that pride has been demonstrated through an enhanced work ethic, not by self-aggrandizement. J. B. Hunt, commenting on the execution of ideas at the company, said that no one at upper management meetings takes credit for decisions. "But the first out of that door is the guy who'd better get it done," Hunt said.[4]

Rates and Margins

Pricing in the trucking industry has been in turmoil since deregulation.

The rate discounts liberally made available by carriers in the 1980s reflected the short-term and frequently irrational marketing strategies followed by many trucking firms. The premise behind discounting was that of differentiating, positioning oneself apart from the crowd. The obvious flaw in this strategy is that giving away something for nothing is not a healthy way to achieve a unique identity.

A similar practice has been followed in trailer utilization. Trailer sizes were increased from forty-five- to forty-eight-foot models during the 1980s, yet carriers continued to charge the same truckload rate they did for the smaller van. And with an increasing use of fifty-three-foot trailers, carriers across the industry have still not adjusted rates for the larger capacity.

Carriers are not only giving away something for nothing, they are all virtually giving away the same thing. Trying to gain a competitive advantage, carriers have ended up in the same relative position as when they started. The problem stems from carriers who set rates without really knowing if they can operate at that level.

"With rate cutting, you'd like to think the guy understood his costs," Bergant said. Hunt, for example, maintained low operating ratios during the 1980s, but it was able to make money at rates that sent other firms into bankruptcy. Before Hunt's operational structure—its corporate fleet, company drivers, and bulk fuel buys—was recognized and copied by other carriers, competitors didn't believe the Arkansas firm could survive the rate discounts. That was another judgment error, Bergant suggested, adding, "You can't make the assumption of rates being a loss leader. You've got to know the company."

Bergant said Hunt set rates by balancing profitability with two marketing perspectives, that of the individual customer and that of the total customer base. Carriers who set rates by single-customer profitability alone lose sight of the bigger picture.

For example, some customers don't provide the profitability Hunt would like, Bergant said, but when placed in a total corporate mix of fifty-five thousand loads a month, these shippers sometimes reveal compensatory advantages, such as being in a strategic location for Hunt to maintain a low empty-mile ratio for its equipment.

Shippers can also influence rates by participating in cooperative efforts such as "driver-friendly freight." Freight can be pre-loaded on pallets and secured with a plastic wrapping to eliminate handling by drivers, warehouse crews, or "lumpers," laborers who work the loading docks.

"Driver-friendly freight gets specialized pricing because when a truck gets unloaded faster we can all save money," Paul James said. "In the past, shippers have had the advantage of driver labor in unloading, and drivers have lost hours in the truck. Less time on the dock means better utilization of our equipment and less fatigue for our drivers. That's good for us and for the customer."

Despite the marketing synergies, rates are about as low as

they can go, or as Thompson said, "the blood is out of the turnip," and all allowances have been made. Hunt margins have declined by more than 50 percent since 1986, and the industry as a whole has been similarly affected. Having been to the bottom in terms of rate structure, and having seen relatively little rate adjustment for inflation, Thompson believes carriers will be more aggressive when setting rates with shippers. Carriers may also have a bit more courage because fewer alternatives are available to shippers than five years ago.

Until recently, fuel surcharges affected most truckload rate increases, offering carriers some opportunity of offsetting huge fuel price swings. But fuel surcharges have not been imposed frequently. A surcharge in the early 1980s lasted almost two years, but that was not repeated until a cold winter in 1990 drove up demand for fuel oil. The third fuel surcharge in more than a dozen years was precipitated by instability in the Persian Gulf following Iran's invasion of Kuwait in 1990. Oil prices rose from sixteen to seventeen dollars per barrel in late July to forty dollars per barrel in September.

Fuel surcharges are permitted by the federal government when volatile and obvious price increases threaten carrier operations. Sometimes, as in the 1980s, a surcharge will be rolled into the allowable base rate. But carriers suffer more when minor upward changes in fuel prices continue over a period of time. A three-cent overnight increase in fuel prices, for example, can cause what Bergant called "creeping margins," a small but consistent erosion of profits that is impossible to recoup.

J. B. Hunt, asked to describe his company's best competitors, might have been describing his own operation when he spoke of a firm that "knows how to price its business, that plans on staying and not getting rich overnight." For Bergant, success in the trucking industry meant surviving shipper consolidation, the reduction from several dozen carriers to only a handful of highly dependable and flexible service-oriented firms. Bergant's assessment was shared by

Chuck Wilkins, director of transportation at Ford Motor Company.

"We're looking for reliable transportation at a reasonable price. This is not a bargain-basement search," Wilkins said. "A low-price company is usually selling available space when it is available. It may not be there when we need it it. Price is important, but we're finding a happy medium of top service carriers."

The ultimate test of survival, Bergant believes, is the ability to provide personalized service in core-carrier relationships. As the freight pie gets cut into larger slices, fewer people will be taking pieces of it, he said.

Core Carriers and Corporate Partnerships

"The customer I prefer is someone who consistently ships high volume with little seasonal or cyclical variation."

Thompson's vision of an ideal Hunt customer sounds like a description most service-company executives would offer. But Thompson took the customer relationship to a more advanced degree by stating the Hunt goal of working with shippers who are "progressive in their partnership relations."

A mutually beneficial relationship entails a great deal more than responding to shipper needs with available equipment and reasonable prices. For Hunt, a progressive partnership requires a thorough understanding of customer logistics—the input of raw materials from suppliers or the dispatching of finished products to regional distributors.

The carrier who can consistently uphold the schedule integrity of that process will be rewarded with continued business. But the carrier who can enhance that process with operational efficiencies and suggestions for mutual improvement will build the partnership relations Thompson identified. The more progressive the relationship, the more likely a carrier will be to survive trucking-firm attrition and be selected as a core carrier.

Providing dedicated equipment is one aspect of building a partnership relation. Hunt has cultivated that service in its automotive division, started in 1987 with approximately fifty loads per week and now delivering nearly four thousand truckloads per week across the country. At its Louisville, Kentucky, terminal, Hunt has dedicated up to 40 percent of its equipment for exclusive service to a nearby Ford Motor Company plant. Hunt's core carrier service to the nation's big three auto makers increased by 11 percent in early 1991 compared to the previous year.

Because of a widespread use of just-in-time manufacturing systems, the automotive industry is particularly sensitive to delivery schedules. With little inventory maintained at vendor or manufacturing sites, freight can go from the truck trailer directly to the plant assembly line. To meet the narrow time frame required by its automotive customers, Hunt established a more frequent driver call-in process than used for its other deliveries. In a worst-case scenario, when the plant is facing a forced shut down because of a late or stranded delivery, Hunt can dispatch another truck to the job. The instant communication ability of Hunt's new satellite system will be of particular value at such times.

"We expect the carrier to act as our representative on the road," Steve Horn, a material planning/analysis supervisor at Ford, said. "We're looking for a carrier who can guarantee delivery in coordination with our material suppliers and our plant need-times."

Ford offers carriers a highly disciplined role in its just-in-time manufacturing process. Carriers are made aware of the locations of Ford manufacturing plants and the suppliers of parts. Carriers must determine transport time between the two sites, maintaining adequate flexibility in equipment to deal with changed schedules at either end. Daily production reports show transit failures, and carriers must account for any setbacks.

Hunt's ability to meet this demanding service requirement earned Ford's 1989 Award for Transportation Excellence, a recognition Horn said was based on a carrier's stability and level and quality of service. Hunt routed 350 moves (a supplier-manufacturing plant link) among Ford's 17 U.S. plants that year, Horn said.

"We'll ship more than a million loads this year, most of it by truck, so we are interested in people who are long-term players," he said. "We're not interested in their leases or default payments. We want to make sure someone will be around."

Horn said Hunt showed an operational advantage over other carriers when selection was based primarily on cost. Now that more sophisticated tracking and analysis equipment has become available, Hunt partnership abilities have become even clearer.

"We're asking carrier partners to help us redefine the way we run transport," Horn said. "Hunt does that better than most. As we continue to use fewer people and better systems, our partners become systems managers for us. That is Hunt's major advantage."

Ford is joined by several other national firms that have selected Hunt as a core carrier. At Champion Paper, which operates ten paper mills across the country, Transportation Director Jerry Loomis said Hunt met the company's criteria of size, service, and price better than any other trucking firm. Delivering 7,285 loads for the company in 1990, Hunt was selected as Champion's Motor Carrier of the Year for the second year in a row. Loomis said Hunt personnel met frequently with his company to explore new opportunities, and he praised the stability shown by the Hunt team.

"My concern is that as a company gets larger and looks to more things, management resources get thin and the customer suffers," Loomis said. "We've been dealing with Hunt for more than five years, and that hasn't happened."

When General Foods Corporation decided to reduce its number of carriers, its first selection criteria was the ability to handle volume traffic in specific geographic areas. With nine plants and fourteen distribution centers, General Foods shipped about two thousand loads a week. The company was looking for a carrier with a national presence to support that volume and a proactive management ability to meet future changes, Dick Hanson, transportation director, said.

"We felt Hunt was trying to modify their service to our needs," Hanson said. "Most other companies, though they say the right things, are not willing to be flexible and tailor their services."

General Foods selected Hunt as a core carrier and assigned it all plant-to-distribution-center traffic lanes. With an adequate equipment resource and an EDI system to facilitate transactions, Hunt has so effectively provided for General Foods' transportation needs, the company is considering expanding the Hunt role to a new phase of service.

"We're now looking at customer deliveries out of our distribution centers and finding ways to get some continuous movement efficiencies through the full supply chain," Hanson said. "Hunt service and pricing will contribute economies as we link the total supply chain on a national scale."

The common theme expressed by Hunt's corporate partners and core relations is that the trucking firm is both innovative and standardized. The business axiom of "grow big but act small" has been demonstrated by a company that is managing growth yet maintaining a small carrier's flexibility. Hunt provides customized service to those customers that can sustain it on a national scale.

Quantum

When Hunt announced its intermodal partnership with the Atchison, Topeka, Santa Fe Railway in December 1989, trucking companies and railroads across the nation were taken by surprise. Intermodal services had been available for some time, but never before had industry players of such national prominence joined together to provide them.

Quantum, the Hunt–Santa Fe partnership linking the

eastern half of the United States and the West Coast through truck-rail services, gained additional attention because it signaled a changing relationship between two fiercely competitive industries. Since 1980 when railroads and trucking were deregulated, both industries had been vying for a common shipper marketplace. Despite the accepted use of intermodal services for containerized freight and trailer-on-flatcar rail service, the prospect of a major rail-motor carrier partnership seemed improbable.

Hunt, of course, had created its trucking business by bringing together what others had seen as completely unrelated parts, and one of J. B. Hunt's essential business skills has always been this type of creative realignment. Some call this entrepreneurial vision. Others view it as the common sense to recognize opportunity. In the rail and trucking environment, it was the ability to see beyond immediate conflict and recognize a common ground.

The announcement of Quantum also forced trucking firms to accept the economic reality of long-haul transport. With a given size and weight capacity of their trucks and an ever-increasing price of fuel, motor carriers had to realize there was little chance for them to compete with railroads in traffic lanes that crossed the western deserts and mountains.

"The long haul, 2,000 mile 'sock the railroads where it hurts the most' type of business is no longer there," William Legg, a transportation analyst at Alex Brown, said. "The railroads have basically won."[5]

Some speculation had risen concerning approval for longer combination vehicles (LCV) as part of the 1991 Highway Bill. Federal approval of twin forty-eight-foot trailers and other LCVs on interstate highways might have helped carriers become more competitive with railroads.

Railroads lobbied hard against that possibility, contending that longer trucks with 134,000-pound weight limits would divert 10 percent of all rail traffic and 16 percent of gross railroad revenues to motor carriers. An official with the American Association of Railroads added to the legislative drama by stating, "We won't be caught unawares. This is a life and death issue for us."[6]

But in the end the Highway Bill only included a fuel tax increase for road construction, defering approval for LCVs to state government. Currently, only a handful of western states permit LCV usage.

Through the 1980s, the rate base for long-haul truckload deliveries decreased faster than short-haul rates. The declining profitability in long-haul lanes should have been a warning of impending change for motor carriers, but most of the industry was too occupied trying to stay in business to pay attention to such details.

"Freight will gravitate toward the most efficient economic mode," Thompson said. "So if the railroad can go seventy-five miles per hour on all welded-rail, double tracks from Chicago to Los Angeles, what makes a trucker think he can compete with that?"

Instead of competitive thinking, truckers should have been considering the more obvious potential of cooperation. According to the American Trucking Associations, intermodal transport had increased by 15 percent in the past decade, and 95 percent of all intermodal movement involved some trucking support. A growing globalization of the marketplace, well articulated in the Hunt 1990 annual report, also lent itself to intermodalism. The potential was already being achieved at West Coast ports specializing in container traffic from Pacific Rim nations. The elimination of trade barriers in North America and western Europe was also contributing to an increasing use of intermodal services.

Yet the traditional rivalries of truckers and railroads kept both parties from acting on these possibilities. Trucking firms exploited the poor service factor of rail transport, reminding shippers that drayage operations, the unloading work at the rail yard, was highly undependable. This was the railroad's recognized weakness. In vast rail yards, freight might require a longer time to unload and deliver than it took to be transported across country.

For their part, railroads promoted the lower cost and unlimited weight capacity of their services. Yet in balance, neither side had a defined advantage because they were primarily dealing with different products and markets. Trucks would not be used to haul coal or other heavy loads, but railroads could not provide the door-to-door service required by shippers.

As is often the case in stalemate situations, an outside mediator can reveal new opportunities for progress. Thompson said the Chicago consulting firm of McKinsey and Company approached Hunt with the idea of an intermodal partnership with Santa Fe. Meeting with the railroad, Thompson said Hunt discovered the two firms had "great chemistry," and business relations were quickly developed.

"We think we have the best sales force and best service in the industry. They think they have the fastest railroad. That's what we're combining," J. B. Hunt said at the press conference announcing Quantum.[7]

Hunt committed 150 trailers to support the initial Chicago-to–Los Angeles service. In February 1990, its first month of operation, Quantum carried forty-three truckloads of freight and generated seventy-two thousand dollars revenue. By the end of the year, Hunt reported that Quantum had been expanded to include San Francisco and Kansas City and activity had increased to one thousand loads per month, generating revenue of two million dollars. In 1991, further expansion included a Dallas–Los Angeles link and Quantum service from the West Coast to the entire eastern half of the country.[8]

The marketing advantages of the partnership were essentially the same for both parties. Santa Fe would have new access to markets beyond the reach of its tracks, which extended from Chicago to the Texas gulf to southern California. Hunt would also have exposure to new customers and be able to offer them more rapid service.

The new customer base Hunt projected for Quantum was not expected to decrease established relations with shippers. Hunt was more active in the short-haul sector and in more densely populated areas of the nation. Smaller trucking firms able to offer deeply discounted rates had a market advantage for long-haul western runs. It was that market share Hunt expected Quantum to capture.

In accord with the corporate marketing strategy for the 1990s, Quantum would compete on quality of service rather than cost. Quantum offered guaranteed forty-eight-hour transit from the Midwest to the West Coast and third morning delivery service with exclusive express lanes to bypass other trucks on on/off ramps. Shipper satisfaction was further assured by an integration of the Hunt and Santa Fe computer systems for total on-line data on all shipments.

By mid-1991, Quantum was apparently still far ahead of its competitors. The April issue of *Container News* magazine said the Hunt–Santa Fe program goes beyond typical intermodalism and "no directly comparable service has emerged."

The rail-truck partnership offered a smooth fit with several aspects of Hunt operations. It allowed extended equipment utilization by keeping older trucks in service, and it contributed to driver satisfaction with short-haul and dedicated runs that brought drivers home more often.

From a long-term perspective, Quantum also positioned Hunt for what some analysts predict as the eventual replacement of the long-haul, coast-to-coast trucking market by rail service. Changing trends in truckload operations may establish more hub-and-spoke systems, with primary terminals dispatching to five-hundred-mile service areas. If these forecasts prove true, Quantum would maintain Hunt's presence in the long-haul sector as other trucking firms abandon it.

Additional Marketing Opportunities

Short-haul and Flatbed Services

The 1990 acquisition of Bulldog Trucking, a Georgia firm specializing in short-haul and flatbed services and van operations, and the 1991 start up of a corporate flatbed division were explained by Hunt as a response to customer demand and lack of industry capacity in those areas.[9]

Forbes magazine, however, offered a less conservative analysis of the expansion, suggesting the new operations would establish Hunt's position to capitalize on the market when the construction recession ended.[10] This advance position is in keeping with the trucking industry's general role as a front runner of the economy. Because trucking deals primarily with the delivery of wholesale items, economic influences often have an impact on the industry before they are widely perceived by the public.

Flatbed trucking, an estimated three-billion-dollar annual market, delivers a large share of roofing and building materials, as well as oversized items that do not fit in a van trailer. Customer demand for such services was very strong, Paul James said, and Hunt committed an initial two hundred tractors and three hundred trailers. Headquartered at Hueytown, Alabama, flatbed division trucks and drivers will travel the forty-eight states and utilize the Hunt terminal system. Transport division sales and marketing staff help meet flatbed customer service needs.

Bulldog Trucking, with established operations in eastern states, brought an additional five hundred trucks and a dozen truck terminals into the total corporate mix. According to a report from Stephens, Inc., the acquisition was made when Bulldog was in default to its bank, allowing Hunt to obtain most of the company's assets.

"Hunt's purchasing power could result in immediate savings of $0.045 per mile," the report stated, "and Bulldog's Operating Ratio could be reduced from 96.9 to 91.7 percent by that savings alone. Improvement in empty miles could make Bulldog highly profitable. Bulldog's short-haul lanes allow good use of older equipment."[11]

Short-haul traffic accounts for more than 50 percent of the nation's truckload freight. With an extremely low driver turnover and the opportunity for using older equipment,

Hunt recognized a market share that far exceeded the initial return Bulldog could offer. With little fanfare, Hunt established a short-haul service at Chicago in July 1990 and made plans for a similar service at New York City the following year. The short-haul market value of the two metropolitan areas was estimated at one billion dollars each annually.

International Markets

Revenue from established operations in Canada and Mexico contributed 4 percent of the corporate total in 1990, but Hunt has pledged to increase its presence toward becoming the dominant provider of transportation services in the areas.

In Canada, where truckload market potential is estimated at five hundred million dollars annually, Hunt serves the provinces of Ontario, Quebec, and British Columbia, delivering more than one hundred truckloads per day in 1990.

In the early phases of the Canadian service, widely exaggerated rumors about harrassment of Hunt drivers and equipment by Canadians were heard through the company.

Hunt took immediate steps to dispel the negative rumors. Training was provided to drivers in border-crossing procedures and other operational details specific to Canada. Drivers who made frequent deliveries into Canada were interviewed and their positive experiences included in corporate communications. Hunt also cooperated with the Canadian Ministry of Transportation following a 1990 Canadian truck strike, allowing a financial review to disprove allegations of price cutting.

The relationship with Canadian trucking authorities, border-crossing officials, and Canadian drivers has greatly improved since these early apprehensions have been resolved.

In Mexico, where the truckload market is estimated at six hundred million dollars annually, Hunt has developed an interlining or through-trailer service role. Mexican trade agreements with the U.S. forbid the entry of foreign-owned trucks, so Hunt trailers have been brought to border-crossing sites where freight is transferred to Mexican vehicles for continued delivery. Hunt de Mexico, a corporate subsidiary established in 1990 as a partnership with the Mexican carrier Fletes Sotelo, is expected to take advantage of growth opportunities afforded by potential free-trade agreements.

The 1992 restructuring of the European market also holds great potential for Hunt, and initial opportunities are being explored. The 1989 annual report mentioned that strategies were being developed to serve the European market and that Hunt had coordinated its first international shipment to France. The 1990 report stated "it's still too early to tell" what transportation role the company would play in Europe, but the report conceded the existence of growth possibilities and strong margins.

J. B. Hunt has spoken privately about his interest in an operational base in southern Spain that could transport freight from north Africa to markets in eastern Europe. He has also talked about the potential for transport services once the English Channel tunnel project is completed. These ideas may be far from any realistic application, but J. B. Hunt's dreams and visions often have a way of coming to life.

Private Fleets

According to a 1985 report from Equitable Securities, the private carriage sector of the truckload market remains "virtually untapped and is ripe for exploitation." The report said Hunt stock was a recommended purchase because the company was well positioned to address that sixty-billion-dollar market.[12] Restating that potential in its 1986 annual report video, Hunt said that nearly two-thirds of all truckload freight is carried by private companies hauling their own goods. The corporate video predicted Hunt would capture a large share of the private fleet market.

"How do we sell to the private fleet shipper?" Thompson said. "We have to convince him that his fleet is not what he thinks it is, that it may not be run all that well."

Hunt may begin working with a private shipper by supplementing existing services, providing the specialized or additional transport the shipper does not have available, Thompson said. Most private shippers realize their transport costs are higher than those available in the open market, but warehouse savings and other factors involved in the logistics can sometimes compensate for the high costs, Thompson said.

Private fleets can also contribute to a company's image of serving their customers. As an adjunct of their primary business, a private fleet's isolated loss factors may not be significant to the company. Bergant believes this factor is eventually overcome when the fleet grows to such size its costs are no longer offset by corporate pride or public relations.

"We'll do a little talking, but usually a company will convince itself that it is time for a change," Bergant said. "We can monitor the situation from afar and see when they make that decision."

Indications that a company is ready to reconsider the status of its private fleet may come with a reduction in the number of its trucks or an increase in the amount of business Hunt is providing to the firm. The opportunity may come through direct contact with a company that says it is ready to change or through a more gradual process.

"In either case, we'll see the telltale signs and be ready to make them an offer they can't refuse," Bergant said.

8

Corporate Strategy

Growth Strategies

The 1989 shareholders' video, with its primary message concerning Hunt's remarkable growth since 1980, may have left some viewers slightly puzzled.

While the video offered a detailed review of corporate affairs and the potential for Hunt to increase its market share within the one-hundred-billion-dollar truckload market, a "cautious" growth agenda was presented. Hunt will seek a 15 to 20 percent growth rate in the years ahead, the video said, an annual rate approximately half what the firm maintained during its peak years in mid-decade.

To dispel any notions that Hunt lacked confidence about its future potential, the video concluded with J. B. Hunt standing before a row of trucks. "Most people think we did good in the 80s, especially the truckers," Hunt says, offering the thumbs-up sign. "But you just watch us in the 90s."

In 1989, the company realized it was about to begin a new phase of growth. While significant opportunities still remained in the dry van truckload sector, the corporate team realized a more diverse approach was required. At the time, however, many of its new involvements were still in the planning stages, not yet ready for public presentation. As a preview of things to come, Hunt and Thompson discussed the concept of management mobility in a column in the corporate newsletter.

"The worst thing a trucking company can be is immobile," the executives wrote. "If a trucking company only has its trucks moving, yet the management never moves into new areas or experiments with new services, that trucking company is essentially immobile."[1]

Industry analysts forecast similar changes in strategy and direction for trucking firms. The long-haul sector was saturated with efficient carriers, and an increased market share was more difficult to achieve in that tougher competitive environment. John Larkin, investor analyst, suggested that progressive trucking firms would explore new markets, seeking more complex options for growth. The days of easy growth were over, Larkin said.

Ginanne Long predicted Hunt would become more of a distribution/transportation company. "Until recently, Hunt insisted it was a dry van company and would stay that way," Long's research report stated. "Now, their business has changed, and in a serious recession, we may see serious changes in the truckload industry. Hunt management is to the point where they can change very quickly. I see them in other areas."[2]

The new risks and challenges facing the company were not isolated from the larger issues of global competition and emerging industrial capacity in foreign nations. According to J. B. Hunt, the immediate impact on trucking, and within a larger perspective, on the American public, was that after a period of prosperity, people would have to work harder to maintain their standard of living. In other words, the status quo would not continue.

As the industry leader, however, Hunt believes it is in the best position to capitalize on these continuing changes.

Having developed a strong balance sheet and a critical mass in equipment, Hunt is able to negotiate from a position of strength that few other trucking firms are able to match.

At a chamber of commerce speech in late 1990, J. B. Hunt said that rising oil prices would force small and inefficient companies out of business, further opening the market to more stable firms. "For J. B. Hunt, this is going to be good," Hunt said. "We can move a truck further on a gallon of fuel than anyone else."[3]

Jones affirmed the corporate advantage from rising fuel costs. The trucking industry would not disappear because of higher oil prices, so the essential issue was not the cost of fuel but its most efficient usage. "Think of fuel on a comparative basis," Jones said. "How well do you use it in comparison to other firms?"

At this time in its history, Hunt is being presented with numerous opportunities. The 1991 focus on diversification and global involvement is the corporate response, but it is a growth strategy Hunt entered with due deliberation. At the 1989 shareholders' meeting, Jones said that concern about earnings volatility has led the company to break with the "successful strategy of grow, grow, grow predominant in the 1980s."[4]

The need for a change in strategic thinking was also expressed by Bergant who said the industry conditions and the internal structure that contributed to Hunt's success no longer existed.

"Our history shows we were able to grow faster than our competitors during the hard times of the 1980s, but we were much smaller then," Bergant said. "When we were high on growth, we added a lot of new customers. Now it's better for us to focus on customers that can provide us with volume."

Corporate growth will continue but not at the same rapid pace, Bergant believes. Hunt's increasing market share will likely be gained by acquisitions that add corporate equipment without putting new tractors on the highways, a strategy that also benefits the trucking industry.

"We have an obligation, both as an adversary and with some common interests, to lead the industry," Bergant said. "In 1990 we raised rates but didn't add trucks. This added some stability to the industry. Everyone else said 'bravo' and did the same thing."

In periods of transition when numerous options are available, the choices a company makes can produce immediate consequences. In a January 1990 issue of *Forbes* magazine, a ten-year review of the trucking/shipping industry highlighted two firms whose new involvements led to serious losses. Ryder Truck Rental, recovering from a 43 percent loss in earnings, spent much of the past year "refocusing on its basic business after serious fiascoes in other service areas." Consolidated Freightways, hurt by its acquisition of Emery Air Freight, saw a 17 percent drop in earnings.

The lesson of these misguided ventures was certainly not lost on Hunt. With the current environment offering a choice of growth through internal means or through acquisition, Hunt has essentially chosen both options. Initiating a controlled evolution of its corporate strategy, Hunt will maintain its major focus in truckload services while entering new markets and assuming a broader role in the transportation industry.

Corporate strategy continues to be opportunistic with a comfortable ability to take risks. Yet a new level of caution has been introduced.

"The cautious part is not that of the traditional bean counter who says 'let's slow down,'" Jones said. "It is risk taking from a calculated perspective. It means we must understand the other points of view before we react or advocate them."

In the 1990 annual report, Thompson identified potential new markets as containers, flatbeds, vans, tanks, and refrigerated trailers, virtually every type of motor carrier activity other than LTL traffic. Dominated by a few carriers and requiring a system for sorting and routing of freight unlike the truckload process, the LTL market does not meet Hunt's criteria for a high margin environment at this time.

Wherever Hunt's growth strategy leads the company, the concept of logistics will play a significant role. Logistics, Bergant explained, requires a level of customer understanding that transcends any single mode of transportation service. Through logistics, Hunt will continue to achieve the objective stated in the 1989 annual report of being an innovative, forward-thinking company, he added.

"In the 1990s, traffic managers will be responsible for moving not just truckload freight but for getting our customers' products to the marketplace in a global economy," Bergant said. "If we want to be a bigger player and offer viable options for our customers in the future, we must understand his needs and find as many solutions as we can."

Customer support through Hunt's mainframe computer is one of the solutions offered. The computer system offers options for competitive trucklines as well. J. B. Hunt said the data system will soon be able to support several trucklines, providing all equipment and software to run their businesses. The company may not choose to develop a data services operation, but the opportunity is available.

"The heart of North American trucking might be in our basement in the next ten years," J. B. Hunt said, referring to a computer vault at corporate headquarters. Hunt believes even greater potential is available for new and expanded relations around the world.

"I know we can leverage this thing here worldwide," J. B. Hunt said. "It may cost us two million dollars to write a computer program here, but the same program can work globally. The big deals are global. People in Europe are dying to do business with us."

Financial Strategies

An understanding of Hunt finances requires more than a summary review of the corporate balance sheet. This was the message behind comments from Richard Holt, an analyst with Prudential Bache, following Hunt's announcement of flat earning for the fourth quarter of 1989.

"The bottom line in this case is what you see is not necessarily what you get," Holt said. "On the surface, things look kind of mundane, but once you get beneath the surface, I think they had a very good quarter."[5]

Holt cited rising fuel costs, tax and interest rates, and the company's aggressive expansion as some of the less obvious influences on earnings, but he maintained that Hunt had gained much control over productivity and operating performance had improved a great deal during the past year.

This was essentially the same message presented by Thompson a year later after 1990 results showed increased revenue and decreased earnings for the second year in a row. Speaking at the 1990 shareholders' meeting, Thompson explained that Hunt's 3 percent rate increase was not able to offset several "uncontrollable factors." In a comparison to 1986, Thompson said that on a per-truck basis driver salaries had risen 15 percent, insurance rates were up 42 percent despite a stable accident ratio per truck, and advertising for driver recruiting was up 60 percent.

"Uncontrollable items not recovered through rate relief have come out of more of the bottom line," Thompson said. "That is why it is now past time for rates to go up. Remember, the whole industry has experienced the same story."[6]

Rate increases, like rate discounts, are not solitary factors a large trucking firm can impose on its customers without repercussions through the industry. Discounting eventually leads to similar price cutting by competitors, while rate increases can isolate a company from market standards and jeopardize customer relations. Although Hunt had given shippers advance notice of its intentions to raise rates, the 1991 increase did not nearly compensate for a decade of rising costs.

Without a consistent ability to impose adequate rate increases, Hunt has focused its financial strategy on cultivating margins within a conservative path of growth. The decision to avoid overcapacity by limiting fleet additions has allowed the company an enviable control of debt and a more flexible selection of how capital will be used.

Jones said most trucking firms maintain a debt-to-equity ratio anywhere between 2 to 1 and 9 to 1. At Hunt, however, the debt-to-equity ratio is 0.5 to 1, a relatively minor part of the total cost structure and one which reduces the impact of interest rates, Jones said. Unused debt capacity becomes a source of capital which, in turn, allows access to current opportunities, he added.

One application of this available capital is the new salary schedule for drivers. Each one-cent-per-mile increase Hunt offers its drivers costs the company approximately six million dollars a year. When the company was smaller, it relied more heavily on bank financing for growth, and in his speeches during that period J. B. Hunt made frequent references to the large loans he was able to secure.

As a firm gains equity, it must be more careful about debt and resist the temptation to overleverage itself in an attempt to increase market share. For J. B. Hunt, that financial strategy is directly equivalent to greed.

"In a lot of big companies, no one cares about anything but 'what I get,' and that's what puts them out of business," Hunt said. "A lot of people only care about how much money we're going to make. They don't understand we're not trying to figure out how many million dollars we can get. That's on the list, but it's down the list, a result of other goals. We're trying to keep greed out of it and be sure everyone pulls their own weight."

Future Strategies

"We want to be a Federal Express. We want to put some distance between us and the competition."[7]

J. B. Hunt's 1988 comment in *Forbes* magazine offers a concise vision of corporate goals. In the few years since then,

Hunt has applied that vision to the practical realities of the truckload market. In the years to come, the same direct approach will likely be followed, enhanced by Hunt's increasing size and financial strength.

"We're in the catbird seat," Thompson said. "We're in good financial shape, with a good mangement team and good, low-cost service. Going into a recession, we have more opportunity than when times are good. No one wants to loan a trucking company money right now, unless you're J. B. Hunt."

Thompson's self-assessment might sound biased, but industry analysts hold the company in equally high regard. John Larkin predicted Hunt would be among the first carriers to expand into a broad range of services, making aggressive moves as other firms withdrew in a recessive economy. Ginanne Long wrote that the opportunity exists for "dominance to become a real factor in the truckload market. Hunt plans to be a dominant player and seems poised to grab the moment."[8]

One source of strength is Hunt's ability to respond to the best acquisition offers, firms with a strong operational base and located in areas of the country with good market potential. New acquisitions can also be selected on the basis of attracting drivers from geographic areas where Hunt does not have a current driver base.

"We're making big deals right now," J. B. Hunt said. "We have all the purchasing power and all the computer power. We've got an abundance of what most people want."

What Hunt said his company wants is the opportunity to control its destiny. Having paid the price for service and for computer support of logisitics, J. B. Hunt is firmly opposed to a return of government control or comprehensive regulation of trucking. As consolidation continues, he expects to see a balanced price structure and a re-emphasis of quality service.

"There may be a need for regulation in some areas,"

Hunt said, "but when regulation comes in, the guy that really wants to go out and do things, he's handcuffed because he doesn't know the right people and can't get the right deal."

Thompson, on the other hand, suggested that regulation would follow political swings from liberal Democrat to conservative Republican. The pendulum is currently swinging toward an open market philosophy, but as rates begin to rise and some shippers become unable to move their freight, government consideration will be made toward a return of trucking regulation, Thompson said.

Regardless of government control or market opportunities, Hunt's future is viewed with unqualified optimism, a sense of enthusiasm attributable to its founding entrepreneur. Bryan Hunt said his father has taught him that success comes from making the proper response to opportunities.

"Dad may come into my office four or five times a week with a new potential project," Bryan said. "If he had the chance to take on just one project, it would be a huge success. Where a lot of people fail is that they take a good idea and treat it with mediocracy, and it's not successful."

Bryan said he disagreed with his father's self-professed role as a corporate cheerleader, someone who inspires activity but does not become involved in making things happen. The company follows through on many of Hunt's ideas and philosophies, Bryan said.

"He stays so far out ahead of the troops that we never catch up with him," Bryan said. "He has always written things down in his little book about where we're going to be in five or ten years. He doesn't dare tell anybody about them five years before because it scares them to death. But he's always been right. He is a cheerleader, but that isn't the end of what he's doing."

Hunt's future direction and growth are closely linked to the vision and energy of its founder. These are qualities that must be institutionalized if the company is to continue beyond the era of J. B. Hunt's leadership. Yet Hunt, approaching the age when many people retire from business affairs, seems to have hit his stride, maintaining a level of activity that might challenge someone half his age.

In a rare moment of leisure, Hunt stood beside the large globe in his corporate office and offered a candid appraisal of his continuing contribution to the firm.

"I'm the visionary," he said. "I'm the guy that's pushing that globe."

The concept of retirement holds no attraction for someone who is already doing exactly what he most enjoys. For Hunt, the present is so rewarding and the future so ripe with potential that past achievements seem to him small in comparison.

"You can go back to my home county and people think we've done great to get this far," Hunt said. "I don't even think we've started. I don't believe anyone around here can even grasp what the future of this company will be in the next forty years."

For J. B. Hunt, satisfaction with one's achievement must never inhibit the original drive that yielded those accomplishments. Hunt has worked to earn the ability to keep on working, not to reach a point where he could walk away from it all. So business success is not the end or the goal of the process. Rather it is the process of achieving that success that holds the greatest fulfillment.

Having lived those values to his personal satisfaction, Hunt's ultimate challenge may be to embody that ideal into a corporate culture that will remain after he is gone. Yet it would be unrealistic to expect thousands of employees to fully accept this philosophy. People work for material gain, and financial achievement will always remain the primary criteria of success.

What must happen at Hunt, therefore, is that the founder's enthusiasm for the process of work must be translated into a work ethic or style that all employees can accept. This is being done through the corporate emphasis on quality. And it is being demonstrated in the confidence and optimism expressed throughout the company.

The future, both near and long term, will undoubtably hold surprises for Hunt. But a transition has already begun to maintain the progressive strategies so closely associated with J. B. Hunt. Thompson, speculating on the corporate future, sounds much like the man he began working for nearly twenty years ago.

"I see us continuing to evolve and becoming a major provider of transportation services in a global arena, not just truckload and the U.S., but a global player in transportation and logistics," Thompson said. "Anything is possible. Anything that involves wheels and the movement of freight is fair game."

9

Personal and Corporate Values

A corporation, like any large-scale gathering, is influenced by the personal values of its leaders. The larger the organization, the more those individual traits must be institutionalized to guard against bureaucracy and a decreasing personal responsibility. Human values somehow get lost in a crowd. As a company extends its operations to include more people at ever-distant locations, the core values of a founding entrepreneur may become diluted in the constant pressure to meet or exceed previous achievement. A shift from quality to quantity is one of the common pitfalls of growth, as if sheer volume output could counterbalance a decreasing level of workmanship or service.

A work force can be inspired to overcome this tendency. Financial incentives are effective, but they are targeted more toward a handful of high achievers than toward the average worker. The qualities of loyalty and pride motivate people to do their best, and the company that best instills those personal values will have the best long-term productivity.

At Hunt, a deliberate attempt is made to uphold standards that might be considered extraneous to specific job performance. A neat driver appearance, for example, is sustained by the company uniform policy as well as by more subtle persuasions, such as the free shoe-shine machine near the driver break room at the Lowell terminal. A photograph of J. B. and Johnelle Hunt hangs on the wall near the breakroom, as it does near driver areas in all company terminals. The photo reinforces the value Hunt places on family relations and personal morality. It suggests that a husband and wife are a team and that family teamwork, particularly for a truck driver, is a basis for success.

These and other values are some of the many lessons J. B. Hunt imparts to the company. They are based on his life and his experiences with people, a series of events that have shaped the company and made it what it is today. So a review of J. B. Hunt's personal values provides strong insight into the corporate values of the company that bears his name.

Here, too, some of J. B. Hunt's personal values—his spontaneity or his sense of financial worth—may seem extraneous to the corporate structure. But J. B. Hunt's complete influence within the organization is impossible to measure. As a founding entrepreneur at the height of his influence and corporate visibility, J. B. Hunt is a willing model, both for people and the values that guide their cooperative strategies. To fully understand the company, one must understand the man.

The Bald Knob Cadillac

One of the many anecdotes J. B. Hunt likes to relate when speaking to new drivers is a story about a shiny new Cadillac he once saw parked outside a truck stop at Bald Knob, Arkansas. Hunt said it was early in his career as a truck driver, and he was driving night runs on two-lane roads through eastern Arkansas. Stopping for coffee, Hunt was immediately attracted to the car. That evening he made a promise to one day own a car just like that gleaming Cadillac. With that goal in mind, he began to save his money.

Hunt tells the story to encourage drivers to set personal goals and impose the self-discipline necessary to achieve them. But the anecdote offers additional insight into Hunt's view of the value of material goods.

"I know it's great to be rich, so I want everyone to be rich," Hunt said in the 1986 documentary "Portrait of America." "It's like fresh air like I've never had before. Now I've got it and I want some of my fellow workers to come up here and breathe some of this good stuff with me."

For Hunt, new cars and other material goods are the rewards of financial success, but he is careful to distinguish between the reward itself and its underlying function as a motivational tool. Once an award is achieved, the motivation it helped create must continue or else a person will lose his or her values, Hunt believes.

"If you survey everyone, people will tell you all they want, but once they can afford those things, the want goes away," Hunt said. "Everyone tries to measure each other with a wealth yardstick. To me, money is only one of many things to make you happy."

Hunt drives a Cadillac these days, but he said he wouldn't purchase a new one unless he received what he considered a fair trade in. He also has been a frequent driver of the corporate limousine, having refused to hire a chauffeur for the vehicle. Equally comfortable behind the wheel of his six-year-old pickup truck, Hunt believes that personal wealth is influenced by what he calls the "laws of the land."

"A guy who gets so rich that he can't find a car or a house good enough for him, he's only got one way to go, and that's down," Hunt said. "You get in trouble when you start using money loosely, as if it doesn't make a difference what things cost or the prices on a menu. With that attitude, you won't be rich long."

Some people see a contradiction in this message and Hunt's personal style. He wears gold cuff links in the shape of dollar signs and has a fondness for high-priced, custom-made boots. These trappings of wealth are misinterpreted, Hunt said.

"To me, the cuff links, the boots are not flashy things," he said. "People think we're high rollers. We're not. A high roller is a guy who gets in the plane and goes to Vegas or the Virgin Islands for a weekend. We don't have any of that here."

"We bought 1,100 new trucks the other day, good trucks but with no fringes or chrome. We just bought a new jet, and it's been sitting in the hangar waiting for the time needed to go. A lot of people look at tools like toys, but here we divide the tools from the toys."

Lessons from the Rich and the Poor

Hunt's appreciation for people has enabled him to find a common ground for conversation with individuals from all walks of life. Never one to shy away from a stranger, Hunt developed an outgoing personality during his truck-driving days when he had to make the most of brief encounters. Hunt said he also learned an important lesson about people from Winthrop Rockefeller.

"I can talk to everyone," Hunt said, "the driver, the mechanic, a guy hitchhiking, or a corporate CEO. Winthrop Rockefeller really helped me through that. When I went into the sod business, I was at his home and around him a little bit." The exposure gave Hunt a new concept of life and a better understanding of the perception people have of the rich.

"I saw the truth of what big is, and from then on, there wasn't any big giants left for me," he said. "The big man is the guy that doesn't know he's big. The guy who thinks he's important is not."

Hunt shares these views with student drivers, expressing

his philosophy on wealth and personal happiness through anecdotes from his early days as a truck driver. He tells of a driver who, trying to impress the patrons of truck stops he frequented, would put many quarters in the jukebox. That same man, now living in near poverty because he threw his money away, earns a meager income by walking people's dogs, Hunt said.

"Does anyone here want to quit throwing his money away and become rich?" Hunt asks the student drivers. "The way to get rich is to get greed out of your heart. Anything above food, clothing, and shelter is wealth. So wealth isn't anything."

Bryan Hunt believes his father has not significantly changed since his early days in poverty, and his personal spending habits are more reflective of someone with relatively limited financial means. With items like cars, a shotgun for his hobby of bird hunting, or even a suit of clothes, J. B. Hunt will constantly seek a deal. A 1991 *Wall Street Journal* article identified those same qualities.

"Johnnie Bryan Hunt is the kind of guy who spends more than $5 million for a second company jet and then wakes an air terminal manager in the middle of the night to demand a discount on plane fuel."

"After treating 40 guests at a restaurant last Labor Day weekend, he demanded and received his 10 percent senior citizen discount on the $500 bill. Refused the same discount on gasoline for his car, he asked the clerk to throw in a free newspaper instead. 'He doesn't want to read the newspaper—he just wants to cut a deal,' said his son, Bryan."[1]

Because it relates to value, not quantity, personal wealth ought not be measured by finances or material possessions, Hunt believes. Nor can personal wealth be assessed by a simple counting.

"It's like walking up to a guy with ten kids, telling him he's rich, and then asking him which one of his kids is he going to sell," Hunt said.

To emphasize his point, Hunt pulled a gold money clip

out of his pocket and began counting off the few bills it contained.

"Wealth is what you got in your pocket," he said. The expression holds as much meaning for him today as it must have during the Depression. Hunt displayed the four one-dollar bills his clip contained and added, "Now what are you going to spend that on?"

A Personal Work Ethic

Hunt's expansive new headquarters, a fifteen-million-dollar structure adorned with palm trees, antique vases, and Italian tile, may offer a contradictory message about the personal work ethic that pervades the company. Compared to its corporate neighbor Wal-Mart, whose headquarter facilities and executive offices feature small paneled rooms with metal desks and plastic stack chairs, the Hunt decor is lavish.

J. B. Hunt justified the new facilities as a means of attracting high-level customers, but the elegant design of the building includes efficient work stations where the fundamental Hunt work ethic is displayed. The message is reinforced here as well, that the rewards of achievement must never interfere with a continuing motivation to work to one's full capacity.

This pragmatism was expressed by Bryan Hunt, who said, "I was taught to get up early and work late, and to be better than my competitor, no matter what I'm doing." J. B. Hunt maintains a similar daily schedule. In 1987, he told the *Arkansas Gazette* a typical day begins at 5:30 in the morning with a Bible reading and a review of his cattle farm.

"I have breakfast with the guy that owns the muffler shop or some guy that's struggling," Hunt said. "And boy, there's a lesson being around people that's struggling because all you got to do is look back a day or two and you can feel that."[2]

Hunt maintains another perspective on his success with two small notebooks kept in the breast pockets of his jacket

The pages of one book are filled with lists of corporate expenses over the years, information such as daily phone and postage bills, daily salary per employee, fuel consumption, and total miles traveled.

In his other breast pocket, Hunt keeps a notebook of future projections. The second booklet, equally worn from handling and filled with similar pencil notes and lists, contains what Hunt calls the "future of this company." Since 1985, he has been compiling his projections with a high degree of accuracy. He identifies patterns of growth in his expense book, and he forecasts new levels of achievement in the projections book.

Hunt maintains this information without a calculator to assist his computations. The ability to carry out this degree of strategic planning would be notable in any individual. For someone without a formal business education, the skill is quite remarkable. For a seventh-grade dropout, the ability is extraordinary.

"You think anyone is smart enough to project that?" Hunt asked. "That comes from every day I ask God for spiritual wisdom. It's a spiritual wisdom I call foresight."

Hunt's personal drive has its roots in the Bible, a body of knowledge he believes directly related to daily decisions.

"If you read the Bible every day, you will finally get on the page where what you're reading today is exactly what you need for the day, almost as if God's secretary printed it one day and you're reading it the next day. This won't happen overnight, but your watches will finally get synchronized."

Hunt has adapted his religious beliefs to a functioning pattern of daily activity. His energy and his daily work load, he believes, have spiritual motivation. That personal fulfillment is displayed through self-confidence and an unfailing sense of optimism.

"Now if you ask my wife what J. B. is doing, she'll say he's killing himself, but if you ask J. B., he'd say he's doing nothing," Hunt said.[3]

Hunt's involvement in the company's strategic planning,

its daily challenges and pace, has seemingly invigorated him all the more. Having succeeded through periods of adversity and worked for people of questionable values, Hunt's personal optimism influences his professional views.

"The life I've got is the best life. I've learned to be happy through all those things," he said. Referring to the 1950s incident when the owner of a trucking company offered twenty-five dollars for anyone to beat him up, Hunt suggested that even working for foolish or insensitive people could be a positive learning experience.

"People like that could have had power, but they didn't because they used it all the time," he said. "Just throwing power around loosely all the time, it won't be long and you won't have any. That's what power is."

Motivating People

J. B. Hunt's personal enthusiasm has been diffused through the company in policies that encourage professional growth and self-motivation. Similar personnel policies can be found in many corporations, but few other companies have a leading role model to personalize these values. Analyst John Larkin described Hunt as the "classic CEO who can articulate a vision and make it happen and make sure everyone enjoys it, views it as a labor of love as he does."

"J. B. is a leader who understands how to get people excited about what they're doing," Larkin said. "He also pats people on the back several times a day and tells them they're doing a good job. Not many CEOs can do that."

Veteran employees recall when Hunt would walk through the facilities and speak to each person he met on a first-name basis. Hunt now says that although he might not have known every employee's name, he would try to find out enough about people to have a brief conversation, to inquire about their home town or their family.

The modern counterpart of those casual conversations is

the Hunt commitment to human values, to creating an environment where people want to work. J. B. Hunt has commented many times that one of his life goals is to have a hundred millionaires working for him by the time he is seventy-five years old. But he also insists that corporate values include more than financial incentives.

"Just paying a guy and not caring what happens to him, that's terrible," Hunt said. "We have the ability to get these people fired up, to work harder, to save more and do more."[4]

Personal motivation begins with an executive understanding of job delegation, that the right work assigned to the right people will create job satisfaction and benefit the company. J. B. Hunt, for example, has said he knows how to start a business but not how to run one.

"A lot of people think that because you're uneducated, you're not going to make it," Hunt said. "And my argument is that guy's got the best chance. If you don't know anything, you've got to hire the best. Put all the best people together and you've got to win."[5]

Hunt also believes that even the most qualified people require a sense of project ownership. When he gets a good idea, Hunt goes to the person he'll rely on to do the job and lets him "pick up the idea and run." The key is getting others in the organization to develop the concept as if it were their own. Hunt said he learned this lesson after designing a truck specially adapted for hauling poultry.

"The man who was to use it never thought it would work," Hunt said. "I finally took a torch and cut it up. And it was the best idea I ever had."[6]

Personal motivation is fueled by the ability to take advantage of opportunity, Hunt believes. By giving people the chance to prove themselves, and as a result help build their personal wealth, Hunt cultivates their initiative and desire to do more. And in the process of earning their reward, people will also develop a better sense of values.

"If you give a person something he doesn't earn, it generally won't last," Hunt said. "If he earns a million dollars, he'll learn how to manage a million dollars instead of just throwing it out the door."

Giving People an Opportunity

Numerous stories can be found through the company about how individuals were given the initiative to do new things or bring a fresh perspective to an on-going problem. Management of J. B. Hunt's extensive bank holdings, One National Bancshares, for example, has been delegated to Bryan Hunt who previous to 1989 held various corporate positions in marketing, personnel, and facilities construction.

Bryan said his involvement with the bank holding company began after initial research convinced him that Little Rock and Hot Springs branches were not being well managed. Bryan said he made several efforts to explain his concern to his father.

"It was the classic deal where you go in about ten times and say, 'Dad, this isn't working,' and on the tenth time he said, 'Well, I've got a new idea. Instead of you coming in here and telling me it isn't working all the time, why don't you take it over and make it work?'"

The offer was made with the inference that J. B. Hunt already had his mind made up, Bryan said. "It was one of those days where he puts his arm around you and you don't know if it's a 'welcome home' or sending you off to war. So I started coming down here [to the Little Rock bank headquarters] on a regular basis."[7]

At the Lowell truck terminal, Donnie Davis has a similar story to tell. Currently manager of one of the firm's largest terminals, Davis had been with Hunt about a year and a half when he was asked to establish a new terminal at Dallas. With only a three-month period to initiate terminal operations, Davis negotiated for land, worked with contractors, and hired drivers and dispatchers.

The initial crew of 57 drivers grew to 170 by the end of

the first year. When space limitations became a problem, Davis was authorized to expand the facility. He purchased an additional fourteen acres, built a larger terminal, and ended his second year of Dallas operations with 360 drivers.

"That was the best accomplishment I ever had," Davis said. "I took over an operation from nothing and left a piece of myself there. My people also felt the terminal was part of them. I guided the operation, but they ran it."

A Leadership Challenge

Despite the corporate emphasis on personal development, one job remains that can't be delegated. It is the catalyst role that J. B. Hunt plays in corporate affairs, an invaluable contribution in itself, yet one the company has no need of duplicating, Hunt said.

"You won't see another J. B. Hunt around here," he said. "We wouldn't give fifteen cents for another guy like me. We need detail people, those that get down and do it."

J. B. Hunt's admission that the company has no need for another person with his capabilities reveals an essential factor of group activity. Organizations eventually impose direction or limits on professional growth. Teamwork demands compromise, yet personal development may sometimes require breaking away to pursue individual goals.

Allowing a person to move on to new responsibilities is the ultimate challenge of leadership. It is a phase of growth Hunt supports because he said it is good for the individual and, in a larger sense, it is good for the organization.

"Many of my peers think I am nuts because of the way I groom my people and then encourage them to find other business pursuits outside of the company," Hunt said. "You must remember that to groom good people to get rich and move on encourages fresh blood and new ideas at Hunt. You can't allocate the entrepreneurial spirit and then try to reign people in. It won't work. So you expect to grow them up and away. That's my greatest reward."[8]

Creative Spontaneity

Spontaneous thinking is a trademark of the creative mind. Those who have spent time with J. B. Hunt recognize this quality in him, an outpouring of ideas, schemes, and visions that few others can match. Dick Kendrick, a Hunt employee during the rice-hull period, recalled a conversation on the topic.

"I was driving with J. B. one day and he said, 'You ever have an idea come through your head and get away before you had the chance to write it down?'" Kendrick said. "I said no, but my ideas are not whistling for the right-of-way in my head like they are in yours."

J. B. Hunt's idea-a-minute style imposes some distraction on the executive team that must assess which of his dreams could become reality and at what cost. According to the *Wall Street Journal,* in recent years the management team has investigated and rejected ideas to build a trailer-manufacturing plant in Arkansas, to put Hunt trailers on barges between Florida and Puerto Rico, to extract oil from old tires, and to sell surplus telephone capacity.[9]

J. B. Hunt's ideas are generally just the initial concept of a large-scale project. His role has been as catalyst for that process, not someone who will address the structural details of making a project work.

"He's not a detail person," Johnelle Hunt said. "He likes to go out and get something, but you take care of it. Once he gets the deal, he's ready to start looking again."

Thompson expanded on J. B. Hunt's noninterest in details, saying his biggest flaw was that he'd rather talk about things than actually do them. Yet Thompson and the Hunt executive team have learned to work well with their sometimes unpredictable chairman. The corporate effort has never been a one-man show, Thompson explained. J. B. Hunt comes up with pieces of the strategic formula, bringing a sense of vision and courage to the planning table, then he leaves good people alone to do their jobs, Thompson said.

J. B. Hunt takes this analysis with a grain of salt. "If you don't put some risk in your business, you'll go broke," he said. "You got to have a little luck and a little faith to go with it."

Admitting that he has become frustrated having to explain things and take people through his ideas, J. B. Hunt views this shortcoming as part of his overall spiritual makeup.

"God doesn't let a guy be creative and have all this detail, too," he said. "God gives man from one to ten gifts. He didn't give us five hundred. You've got to work on the one he gave you."

Conclusion

The generous soul will be made rich.
Proverbs 11:25

From the windows of his fourth-floor office at the Hunt corporate headquarters, J. B. Hunt can look out on the rolling hills of northwest Arkansas, a landscape similar to the countryside where he was raised. A little more than two hundred miles separate the corporate chairman from the provincial locale of his youth, but few would deny that Hunt has traveled great distances in the four decades since he left Cleburne County with ten dollars in his pocket and the hope of finding a job.

He has returned to the area many times, but no occasion may have held greater significance than a spring evening in 1987 when Hunt was asked to deliver the commencement address at West Side High School at Greers Ferry. The seventh-grade dropout was introduced to the graduates as a man who got his start selling wood chips for chicken litter.

He told the graduates that they had taken the first step to becoming rich, but he warned them that wealth would not mean much if they forgot other things—"like the Lord Jesus Christ," he said.

He admonished them to work hard and fast.

"Don't wait around for your grandfather to die and leave you a few bucks," he said. "Nobody is going to give you anything."

J. B. took some time to talk directly to the men.

"I teach a class to my truck drivers on how to get along with your wife," he said, going on to offer them a few jewels from the curriculum.

"Unless you find someone you can't live without," he said, "don't marry her."

He told them to plan on marrying only one woman and staying with her the rest of their lives.

"And tell your wife you love her," he said. "I tell Johnelle I love her twice every day."

Johnelle was in the audience. She nodded approvingly.[1]

Hunt's homecoming underscores his lifelong belief that ordinary and even limited origins are no barrier to extraordinary achievement. His personal achievement illustrates the essential values of marriage and spritual belief. In his personal life, as in his business affairs, Hunt has lifted the commonplace to new heights and revealed its intrinsic worth, a resource often overlooked in the pursuit of wealth and happiness.

Calling himself a "Christian who attends a Baptist church," Hunt believes in divine intervention, and he credits his life successes and failures to God. Errors and misjudgements, as much as his foresight and accurate decisions, are part of that divine guidance, he believes.

"Everything bad that has happened to me, at that point in time was turning me," Hunt said. "If it hadn't happened, I'd have gone right off the cliff. God is not going to let you be 100 percent every day. Something bad happens, that's for a reason. I go on. I don't brood over it."

Hunt rarely reflects on the past. His sense of achievement stretches out ahead of him like an open road. The result is a personality Kirk Thompson described as the "most consumate optimist I've ever met."

Thompson also commented, as have many others who know the Hunts well, that J. B. Hunt has been a visionary, but it is Johnelle Hunt who has provided a realistic perspective to his spontaneity, serving as the "reins on a wild horse" for his challenging ideas.

Johnelle's religious convictions are as deeply held as J. B.'s, and she has chosen a role of supporting partner to her husband's lead efforts. Yet from that position she has influenced many of their business decisions. Johnelle has maintained a full-time involvement since the start-up of the rice-hull plant. Gene George, a corporate director for more than thirty years, called Johnelle the most important factor in Hunt's success.

"Many times I've told J. B. that it's Johnelle, not him, making the right decisions," George said.

J. B. Hunt understands the problems and pressures his wife has endured, particularly in the years when he was away from home for long periods.

"Somebody has to pay the price of being successful, and it's normally not the guy who deserves the credit. It's his wife and family," Hunt said. "You better have a good wife when you start down a fast road because if you don't, you're not going to make it."

Like J. B., Johnelle does not dwell on the past, but she will talk about the early efforts and difficulties including details J. B. does not recall. She said her roughest time as a truck driver's wife was when their newborn son Bryan was hospitalized and in critical condition with a lung infection. J. B. was unable to quit driving and spend time with them, she said.

"I was there where it was happening, but he had to get on the truck and go out every day," she said. "It was probably harder on him than on me. That was a real tough time. Years later you look back and realize how fortunate you were."

Johnelle also speaks about the good balance between her and J. B. She has asked for explanations of how ideas and new business schemes would work, and she has gotten J. B. to slowly explain his thoughts, an accomplishment of no small order.

"The main problem is you hear it for the first time, but he's been thinking about it for a while," Johnelle said. "He's about twenty steps ahead of me, so I hear it and think it won't work."

Johnelle has expressed her lack of confidence in some projects, but she has always gone along with her husband when "he was that sure and determined." In this role, she has found a personal fulfillment as a wife and partner, and she has gained wide respect from their business associates.

J. B. and Johnelle Hunt have created a business, a family, and a tradition of caring for people. And they have done so with the most basic tools possible. The result of these actions has been a material wealth that few can equal and a spiritual wealth displayed in their everyday interactions.

A wall plaque outside the front doors of the Hunt corporate headquarters contains three Bible verses, including Proverbs 11:25, "The generous soul will be made rich." In recent years, the Hunts have begun to receive the recognition to prove that phrase true. They were Arkansas Easter Seals' 1990 Arkansans of the Year. And when the Arkansas Motor Carrier Hall of Fame was established in 1991, J. B. was named its first inductee.

Some people might believe a conflict exists between the competitive world of big business and the spiritual and human ethics of religious values. J. B. and Johnelle Hunt have reconciled the two.

J. B. HUNT CORPORATE HISTORY MATRIX

	Revenue	Revenue Percent Change	EPS	Stock Splits	Earnings	Total Trucks	Total Trailers	Total Drivers	Total Personnel	Operating Ratio	Total Miles Traveled	Average Miles Per Tractor	Empty Mile Factor
1961	100,000				(19,123)				5				
1962													
1963	147,197				26,089								
1964	184,661	9			14,893								
1965	216,630	17			14,414								
1966	263,908	22			26,995								
1967	457,036	73			37,907								
1968	429,823	-6			18,189								
1969	827,198	92			51,550	5	7		19				
1970	1,966,199	138			38,841								
1971	2,762,728	41			81,334								
1972	2,478,406	-10			(141,933)								
1973	3,710,798	50			(53,242)								
1974	3,319,012	-11			169,932								
1975	3,466,109	4			136,543								
1976	4,203,066	21			186,509								
1977	6,517,832	55			333,214				127				
1978	10,156,259	56	.03		388,000	89	123		209	92.7	8,161,000	116,586	10.5%

Year													
1979	14,693,000	45	.08	3–2	546,000	241	474		459	89.3	17,796,000	117,079	9.2
1980	25,298,000	72	.08		(10,000)	239	426		419	92.6	27,270,000	107,787	9.7
1981	30,534,000	21	.22		2,046,000	265	444		436	90.9	29,669,000	123,108	9.1
1982	40,301,000	37	.35	2–1	3,483,000	368	770		649	85.0	39,914,000	127,929	8.5
1983	63,024,000	56	.39	5.83–1	8,437,000	550	1,049	787	1,050	78.6	62,173,000	135,339	6.76
1984	97,945,000	55	.64		14,141,000	833	1,450	1,100	1,453	75.9	95,231,000	138,572	5.22
1985	131,475,000	34	.70		16,314,000	1,236	2,468	1,676	2,291	79.7	128,544,000	130,484	5.42
1986	203,786,000	55	1.05	2–1	24,738,000	1,957	3,819	2,775	3,665	77.1	200,042,324	131,930	5.83
1987	286,419,000	41	1.10		25,971,000	2,544	5,718	3,835	5,155	85.0	286,477,000	131,771	5.91
1988	392,553,000	37	1.40		33,045,000	3,135	7,071	4,755	6,466	84.8	382,743,000	131,800	5.40
1989	509,278,000	30	1.30		30,615,000	4,096	9,339	5,346	7,380	87.9	495,377,000	130,020	5.85
1990	579,831,000	12	1.28		30,048,000	4,729	10,563	6,291	8,478	90.2	541,079,000	128,010	5.97

NOTES

All direct quotations in this text, unless otherwise indicated, were obtained from the author's personal interviews with the subjects. The interviews were conducted in the summer and fall of 1990.

Introduction

1. *Arkansas Business,* September 26, 1988.

1. Corporate History to 1980

1. *Arkansas Gazette,* September 9, 1990.
2. *Arkansas Democrat,* August 25, 1961.
3. *Arkansas Democrat,* May 16, 1962.
4. *Arkansas Gazette,* April 5, 1987.
5. *Arkansas Gazette,* April 5, 1987.
6. Arkansas Easter Seals, *Arkansans of the Year* video, 1990.
7. *J. B. Hunt Company Annual Report, July 1962.*
8. Cushman, Darby, and Cushman (Washington, D.C., patent attornies) letter, September 12, 1966.
9. *Arkansas Gazette,* April 5, 1987.

10. *Arkansas Gazette*, April 5, 1987.
11. *Arkansas Democrat*, February 28, 1971.
12. *Arkansas Democrat*, April 10, 1971.
13. J. B. Hunt Company board of directors meeting notes, May 15, 1974.
14. *Arkansas Poultry Times*, February 24, 1971.
15. J. B. Hunt Company board of directors meeting notes, November 21, 1975.
16. J. B. Hunt Company board of directors meeting notes, May 1, 1977.
17. J. B. Hunt Company board of directors meeting notes, November 4, 1977.
18. J. B. Hunt Company board of directors meeting notes, June 10, 1978.

2. Deregulation and the Modern Trucking Industry

1. Glaskowsky, Nicholas, *Effects of Deregulation on Motor Carriers*, Westport, CT, Eno Foundation, 1990, p. 11.
2. Winston, Clifford, Thomas M. Corsi, Curtis M. Grimm, and Carol A. Evans, "Deregulation's Losers and Winners: Measuring the Effects," *The Private Carrier*, July 1990.
3. Derthick, Martha, and Paul Quirk, *The Politics of Deregulation*, Washington, DC, The Brookings Institution, 1985, p. 29.
4. Derthick, p. 46.
5. American Trucking Associations, *American Trucking Trends 1989*, Alexandria, VA, 1989, p. 30.
6. Glaskowsky, p. 44.
7. Dempsey, Paul Stephen, *Social and Economic Consequences of Deregulation*, Paul Stephen Dempsey, 1988, p. 95.
8. *New York Times*, October 8, 1986.
9. *Fortune*, March 30, 1987.
10. *USA Today*, October 25, 1990.
11. Dun and Bradstreet Failure Data, 1978–1988, published in *American Trucking Trends*, 1989, p. 30.
12. Interview with Ken Seigel, ATA Information Services, November 1990.
13. Glaskowsky, pp. 16–20.
14. Crum, Michael, and Benjamin Allen, "Shipper EDI, Carrier Reduction, and Contracting Strategies: Impacts on the Motor

Carrier Industry," *Transportation Journal*, vol. 20, no. 4, 1990.
15. Johnson, James C., and Kenneth Schneider, "A Decade After the 1980 Motor Carrier Act: Trucking Company CEOs Discuss Surprises and Speculations," *Transportation Quarterly*, July 1990.
16. *Transport Topics*, June 18, 1990.
17. *Transport Topics*, January 22, 1990.
18. *Arkansas Gazette*, August 7, 1989.
19. *Transport Topics*, January 22, 1990.

3. Corporate History Since 1980

1. Johnelle Hunt, letter to George Reynolds, July 9, 1981. George Reynolds collection, UALR Archives, Little Rock.
2. Arkansas Easter Seals, *Arkansans of the Year* video, 1990.
3. *Business Week*, May 27, 1985.
4. Equitable Securities research report, December 26, 1985.
5. *Merrill Lynch Research Comment*, October 21, 1985.
6. *Business Week*, May 26, 1986.
7. *Forbes*, November 4, 1986.
8. *Arkansas Gazette*, December 2, 1986.
9. *Business Week*, May 26, 1986.
10. *Arkansas Gazette*, April 5, 1987.
11. *Arkansas Democrat*, February 1, 1987.
12. *OTC Review*, July 25, 1987.
13. *OTC Review*, September 9, 1987.
14. *Forbes*, October 26, 1987.
15. *Arkansas Gazette*, August 20, 1987.
16. *Arkansas Democrat*, April 29, 1987.
17. *Arkansas Business*, September 26, 1988.
18. *Business Week*, October 21, 1988.
19. *Arkansas Gazette*, January 9, 1989.
20. *Arkansas Gazette*, March 5, 1989.
21. *Arkansas Democrat*, March 3, 1989.
22. *Arkansas Gazette*, March 1, 1989.
23. *Arkansas Gazette*, May 3, 1989.
24. *Arkansas Democrat*, May 3, 1989.
25. *Arkansas Democrat*, July 13, 1989.
26. *Arkansas Democrat*, December 14, 1989.
27. *Distribution*, July 1990, and *Transport Topics*, August 13, 1990.

28. *Forbes,* January 7, 1991.
29. *Transport Topics,* August 13, 1990.
30. *Arkansas Democrat,* February 2, 1990.
31. *Arkansas Democrat,* May 2, 1990.
32. Stephens, Inc., research report, August 30, 1990.
33. *Changing Lanes* (J. B. Hunt newsletter), February, 1991.
34. *Forbes,* November 26, 1990.
35. *Arkansas Democrat,* January 25, 1991.

5. Operations

1. Crum, Michael, and Benjamin Allen, "Shippper EDI, Carrier Reduction, and Contracting Strategies: Impacts on the Motor Carrier Industry," *Transportation Journal,* Summer 1990, vol. 29, no. 4.

7. Marketing

1. *J. B. Hunt Transport Services, Inc., 1990 Annual Report,* p. 8.
2. *Arkansas Democrat,* December 14, 1989.
3. *Arkansas Democrat,* February 1, 1987.
4. *Arkansas Business,* September 26, 1988.
5. *Transport Topics,* January 22, 1990.
6. *Journal of Commerce,* November 1, 1990.
7. *Arkansas Gazette,* December 13, 1989.
8. *Changing Lanes* (J. B. Hunt newsletter), November 1990.
9. *Arkansas Gazette,* November 6, 1990.
10. *Forbes,* November 26, 1990.
11. Stephens, Inc., research report, August 30, 1990.
12. Equitable Securities research report, December 26, 1985.

8. Corporate Strategy

1. *Customer Matters* (J. B. Hunt newsletter) July 1989.
2. Stephens, Inc., research report, August 29, 1990.
3. *Arkansas Democrat,* October 11, 1990.
4. *Arkansas Democrat,* May 2, 1990.
5. *Arkansas Democrat,* February 2, 1990.

6. *Changing Lanes,* February 1991.
7. *Forbes,* December 12, 1988.
8. Stephens, Inc., research report, August 30, 1990.

9. Personal and Corporate Values

1. *Wall Street Journal,* May 9, 1991.
2. *Arkansas Gazette,* April 5, 1987.
3. *Portrait of America* video, 1987.
4. *Portrait of America* video, 1987.
5. *Arkansas Gazette,* April 5, 1987.
6. *Arkansas Business,* September 26, 1988.
7. *Arkansas Gazette,* March 25, 1991.
8. *Rare Breed,* p. 71.
9. *Wall Street Journal,* May 9, 1991.

INDEX

Hunt, Walter and Alma, 1–2, 4
Hunt, Wilburn, 2, 4
Hunt de Mexico, 56, 119

IBM, 94
IBM Software-Defined Network, 94
Interstate Commerce Commission (ICC), 21, 22–23, 24, 28, 29, 33, 39
Illinois, 4, 17
Initial Public Offering, 43
International Harvester, 76, 86
Interstate 20, 75
Interstate 30, 65, 75
Iowa, 17

James, Paul, 78, 80, 85, 107, 117
J. B. Hunt Company, ix, xi, 11, 12, 15, 17, 19
J. B. Hunt Transport, ix, x, xiii; 1990 annual report, 59; flatbed division, 56–57, 116–18; logistics division, 52, 100–04; marketing division, 104–20; transport division, 21, 81
Jones, Bruce, 37, 54, 78, 103, 105–06, 123, 124, 127
Juarez, Mexico, 57

Kahn, Alfred, 30
Kansas City, 115
Kendrick, Dick, 143
Knapp, Larry, 89–90

Larkin, John, 41, 46, 52, 122, 128, 139
Legg, William, 113
less-than-truckload (LTL) carriers, viii, 27–28, 30, 34, 35, 36, 39, 43, 57, 88, 124
Little Rock, Arkansas, 5, 7, 8, 9, 11
Long, Ginanne, 51, 55, 122, 128
longer combination vehicles (LCV), 113–14
Loomis, Jerry, 111

Los Angeles, California, 115
Louisville, Kentucky, truck terminal, 110
Lowell, Arkansas, ix, 19, 20, 24, 48, 50, 53, 89, 105
Lufkin Company, 86

Maestri, Paul, 18
Malcolm Baldridge National Quality Award, 98
McKinsey and Company, 115
Merrill Lynch, 45
Ministry of Transportation, 118
Minnesota, 17
Mississippi County, Arkansas, 2
Missouri, 4, 17
Morgan Keegan, 48
Morgan Stanley, 51
Motor Carrier Act of 1935, 28
Motor Carrier Act of 1980, viii, 21, 28
Motor Carrier of the Year, 111
Motor Carriers Lawyers Association, 29

Navistar International, 48, 86
New York City, 56, 118
North Little Rock, Arkansas, 45

on-board computers (OBC), 95
"One Hundred Fastest Growing NASDAQ Companies," 48
"One Thousand Most Valuable Companies," 53
Ontario, 118
Operation North Pole, 80
OTC Review, 48
Ozment, John, 100–01

Palmer, Steve, 97
Peterson, Lloyd, 20
Peterson Industries, 11
Petery, Andras, 51
Pfizer and Co., 19, 20
Pioneer Foods, 23
Portland, Oregon, 61

"Portrait of America," 134
Preferred Automated Customer Exchange (PACE), 95–96
Project Alliance, 78
Project Horizon, 80–81
Prudential Bache, 54, 126

"Quality in Motion" campaign, 98
Quantum, 52, 61, 88, 112–15
Quebec, 118

Ralston, Bob, 82, 87, 88
Ralston Purina, 21
Rare Breed, 89
Red River Feed Company, 5
Reynolds, George, 10, 11, 13
Reynolds Metals, 96, 97
Rio Grande valley, 23
Roadway, 30
Rockefeller, Winthrop, 9, 15, 135
Rogers, Arkansas, 19
Ryder Truck Rental, 124

Sanderson, Tom, 95–96
San Francisco, California, 115
Santa Fe Railroad (Atchison, Topeka, Santa Fe) 52, 112–16
Schneider Truck Lines, 51
Seattle, Washington, 61
Shell, Bob, 8, 44
Simpson, J. D., 43
Snyder, Ivan, 25–26
Staggers Act, 29
Stephens, Bill, 21
Stephens, Inc., 43, 51, 55, 117
Stier, Candy, 75
Stier, Mike, 62–76
St. Louis, Missouri, 52
Stuttgart, Arkansas, ix, 10, 11, 13, 18, 19, 20, 43
Sullivan Associates, 22
Superior Forwarding Company, 8, 9, 10, 11

Surface Transportation Assistance Act, 42
Swift, 5

Teamsters Union, viii
"The Scandal of Killer Trucks," 32
Thompson, Kirk: corporate strategy, 41, 51, 53, 55–59, 85–86; and deregulation, 35; and dress policy, 82; EDI, 96; executive role, 39, 45, 46; on ideal customer, 109; and industry regulation, 129; initial position, 24–25; management, 122; management training 97; and private fleet sales, 119–20; and rail-based freight, 114; and rates, 108, 126; and strategic position, 48, 128, 131
Traffic World, 34
Transportation Journal, 95
Transport for Christ chapels, 83
Transport Topics, 35, 37, 53, 54
Trip Master computers, 48
Truckstops of America, 98
"200 Best Small Companies in the US," 45
Tyson Foods, 11

Unical Systems, 99

Value Line, 48

Wall Street Journal, 136, 143
Watts, Charlie, 79–80
West Side High School (Greers Ferry, Arkansas), 145
Whitman, Lonnie and Tom, 91
Wilkins, Chuck, 109
Winrock Enterprises, 9–11, 13, 15–16
Winrock Grass Farm, 9, 15
Wisconsin, 17